THE LION AND THE BULL

THE LION AND THE BULL

THE GOSPELS
OF MARK AND LUKE

Henry Wansbrough

DARTON·LONGMAN+TODD

226.3

First published in 1996 by
Darton, Longman and Todd Ltd
1 Spencer Court
140–142 Wandsworth High Street
London SW18 4JJ

ISBN 0–232–52162–X

A catalogue record for this book is available
from the British Library

Phototypeset in 10½/13pt Bembo by Intype London Ltd
Printed and bound in Great Britain by
Redwood Books Ltd, Trowbridge, Wiltshire

CONTENTS

Part III **Luke: the gospel of the Spirit**

FOREWORD

This book was written as course booklets for courses in two successive years on the gospels of Mark and of Luke, sponsored by the Union of Monastic Superiors. The participants gathered for some initial lectures, and then departed with the booklets and studied on their own. The questions at the end of each chapter were intended as the basis of essays which were then sent in for comment; but they will still be useful as a focus for private study.

The book is obviously not intended as a continuous commentary on the text of the two gospels: rather it is a series of snapshots or of probes on particular topics. I hope these will give an orientation which will guide the reader into a deeper understanding of the approaches of Mark and of Luke, giving insights into their message, and so making it easier to read and appreciate the Good News which they bring.

Some justification should be given for the topics chosen and the order in which they are presented. First comes the context provided by the world in which the two evangelists wrote. Then there is a brief consideration of the so-called 'Synoptic Problem', to justify taking Mark as the first gospel and Luke as dependent on Mark and Matthew: this hypothesis is the presupposition of all that follows.

Specifically on Mark, a preliminary chapter investigates the methods and literary techniques which are characteristic of Mark and which constitute, so to speak, his personal fingerprint. Why Mark should have written at all is the question next posed; if a book is provoked by some special circumstance, the reader will understand it better against that background. Then two central concerns of Mark's gospel are discussed; the Good News of the kingship of God, and the gradual discovery of the person of Jesus.

Finally in the section on Mark come two special treatments: the first is a consideration of the climax of Mark's gospel, to which everything has been tending, the Passion Narrative. The second is the question which has imposed itself with increasing urgency as we have constantly considered Mark's view of Jesus: is this view a distortion?

In the case of Luke it seemed better to discuss first why he wrote, before fingerprinting him. Next follow two chapters on the Spirit, so important in Luke's double volume, and a further chapter on the themes which reflect Luke's chief concerns in his work of presenting the message of Christ. Finally, there are four chapters on particular parts of his gospel – the parables, the Passion, the Infancy Narrative and the stories of the Resurrection Appearances.

This book does not discuss such topics as the colour of the evangelists' hair (if any), nor the date at which they wrote their gospels. Neither of these add much to our understanding of their message. If you wish to think of Mark's gospel as written between 65 and 75, and Luke's ten years later, I have no objections. (See page 139, where the dating of the gospels is discussed.)

I am grateful to Sister Zoë of Turvey Abbey for suggesting that I should undertake this work, and to the score or so of monastic participants on each course; their essays were stimulating and often challenging. The essays showed that prayer and critical study complement rather than undermine each other.

HENRY WANSBROUGH
Michaelmas 1995

BOOKS

It is essential to have something else to read, to fill out and to clarify this book. I would suggest, in order of priority:

General
The New Jerusalem Bible, London, Darton, Longman & Todd, 1985 – if possible the study edition (1994). The introductions and footnotes provide wide-ranging historical and theological help.

Stanton, Graham N., *The Gospels and Jesus*, Oxford, Oxford University Press, 1989. This has a good, clear introduction to many gospel topics.

On Mark
Hooker, Morna, *The Gospel According to St Mark*, London, A. & C. Black, 1991. This offers manageable commentary on the whole gospel.

Nineham, D. E., *Mark* [Pelican Gospel Commentary, 1963], Harmondsworth, Penguin, 1969. Though obviously an old book, and written primarily for non-Christians, it is still full of wisdom.

On Luke
Goulder, Michael D., *Luke – A New Paradigm*, Sheffield, Sheffield Academic Press, 1989.

Green, Joel B., *The Theology of the Gospel of Luke*, Cambridge, Cambridge University Press, 1995.

Fitzmyer, Joseph A., *The Gospel according to Luke*, New York, Doubleday, 1979.

Caird, G. B. *Saint Luke*, Pelican, 1963.

Talbert, Charles H., *Reading Luke*, London, SPCK, 1982.

On particular topics
Senior, Donald, *The Passion of Jesus in the Gospel of Mark*, Leominster, Herefordshire, Gracewing, 1984.

IMPORTANT NOTE

**Throughout this study it is essential
to read the text whenever a reference is given,
and to become as familiar as possible
with the whole text of Mark and of Luke**

PART I

The context of the gospels

CHAPTER I

BEFORE THE GOSPELS

1 THE JEWS IN THE MEDITERRANEAN WORLD

An alien race in a unified world

From the time of the Babylonian Exile (587 BC), the Jews became scattered round the Mediterranean world. They stood out from other people because of their strange habits. As the Mediterranean world became more homogeneous, first under one empire, then under another, they stood out more and more.

First Alexander the Great (died 323 BC) created an unprecedently vast empire which spread all over the eastern Mediterranean from Greece round to Egypt and as far east as Afghanistan. This whole area developed a single culture, known as 'Hellenistic' from the Greek word for 'Greek'. The same cults, theatres, temples, and designs of cities are to be found everywhere. Everywhere a reasonably good standard of Greek was spoken, less sophisticated and delicate than the classical Greek of fifth century Athens, but still at its best a cultivated and distinguished literary language. Communication over the whole area would have been easy, for the same language and books would have been familiar everywhere.

After Alexander's death, his empire was divided between three generals. It eventually became three empires, the Macedonian, the Syrian (or Seleucid, because the kings were descended from Seleucus), and the Egyptian (or Ptolemaic, because the kings were descended from Ptolemy). Palestine lay between these two latter empires and was dominated first by one, then by the other, depending on which was more powerful at the time.

In 167 BC the Syrian king Antiochus IV Epiphanes attempted to suppress the peculiarities of Judaism within his kingdom, and particularly in Palestine. He was called 'Epiphanes' because, like a number of eastern monarchs at this time, he claimed to be a god, or at least a manifestation of a god ('epiphany' means 'appearance' or 'manifestation'). He attempted to stop the Jews practising all their strange habits: to stop circumcising their male children; to start eating pork; to give up their strange, barbaric, mountain God, Yahweh, who would accept no other god beside him; and to embrace the many gods of the Greek world.

The Greek world had a god to preside over every activity – Artemis for hunting, Hephaistus for metalworking, Cybele for agriculture, Ares for war, and so on – while the Jews had only one God. The Jews were a nation apart, because all the public activities, such as plays in the magnificent open theatres (many of which still stand today) or the Olympic and other Games, involved sacrificing to these gods, and so were closed to the Jews. In addition competitors in the Games were always naked, which the Jews thought shameful; and in fact the Jews' sexual morals and family life were a good deal healthier than those of the Hellenistic world. Then there was the curious Jewish custom of observing one day in seven – the week did not exist as a division of time in the Hellenistic world – as sacred to their God, and refusing to work or to engage in most activities. If the Jews were to be integrated into Antiochus' empire, it was essential that they should abandon this separatism.

Antiochus failed, largely due to the resistance spearheaded by a priestly family from Modein, on the coastal plain, who later became known as the Maccabees (or 'Hammers'). They soon formed the first dynasty of Jewish rulers since the Exile, and achieved for Palestine a large measure of independence from Syria. They were followed by the Hasmonean kings, who ruled the country until Pompey the Great overran it in 66 BC. By then they had enjoyed nearly a century of independent existence.

Palestine under Roman rule

During Pompey's campaigns in the East he used the services of Antipater, an Idumaean (from the territory south of Judaea), as purveyor of supplies to his armies. Antipater became rich and influential, and eventually became the native ruler under Rome. His son, Herod, was appointed king in 40 BC. He was a friend of the emperor, Augustus, and the Romans envisaged his task as being to introduce Roman civilisation into the backward territory of Judaea.

To this there was fierce resistance, and Herod, despite his title of

King Herod the Great, was intensely disliked by the Jewish religious authorities. For one thing, he was only half a Jew (on his mother's side); for another, he was known to sit very loose to the Jewish Law, at any rate outside Judaea. From his immense wealth he made great donations to the cities with large Jewish communities – he paid for the streets of Ephesus to be paved with marble – and he also built standard Hellenistic public buildings in Jerusalem, such as a theatre and a racecourse. He was also responsible for building the magnificent Tomb of the Patriarchs which still stands at Hebron, and above all the splendid Temple of Jerusalem. So grandiose was this Temple that the Roman writer Pliny the Elder says it made Jerusalem 'far the most distinguished city of the East'. He also built fortified palaces in his kingdom, including his winter palace at Massada and his summer palace at the Herodium near Bethlehem, whose ruins still show traces of their splendour and wealth. They were built in the Roman style, but the surviving frescoes show that he was careful to avoid offending Jewish religious susceptibilities: the paintings are 'aniconic', avoiding all representations of humans or animals (in accordance with the current interpretation of the prohibition in the Law of graven images), and employing only geometric and floral designs.

At his death in 4 BC his kingdom was divided between his four surviving sons, who were named 'tetrarchs' (each being the ruler of a quarter). Judaea and its capital, Jerusalem, were allotted to Archelaus, but Archelaus proved himself such a disastrous ruler that after ten years he was deposed and replaced by a Roman prefect. The High Priest continued to exercise a great deal of administrative power, but always under the supervision of the Roman governor. Symbolically, the high-priestly vestments were kept in the custody of the governor, and one after another the High Priests were deposed because they were unsatisfactory to the Romans. Their activity as local rulers was therefore strictly controlled. During the ministry of Jesus, however, the High Priest was Caiaphas, whose term of office lasted nearly twenty years, the last decade of which was during the governorship of Pontius Pilate. There must have been a fair understanding between the two of them.

Of the Roman governors we know most about Pontius Pilate. The Jewish historian Josephus and the Jewish philosopher Philo of Alexandria both characterise his rule as tyrannical and unjust. He was eventually deposed by the Roman governor of Syria (his local superior) in AD 36 for his ruthless overreaction to a messianic revolt in Samaria. However, only limited credence can be placed in the accounts of Josephus and Philo: both had a vested interest in exaggerating the harshness of the Roman regime in Judaea, and so excusing the Jewish reaction to it.

There had been minor insurrections against Roman rule in Palestine before this, but from now onwards resistance stiffened and became more and more violent. Armed resistance was led by the Zealots, and eventually a full-scale revolt broke out in AD 66. Rome reacted strongly, bringing armies to besiege Jerusalem, and in AD 70 the city was captured and the magnificent Temple was sacked. Of the three important groupings of the Jews, the Sadducees, the Pharisees and the Zealots, only the Pharisees survived as a party. They re-formed at the city of Jamnia on the coastal plain, under the leadership of a Galilean rabbi, Yohanan ben Zakkai, reasserting and codifying the traditions of the Law. It is from there that the tradition of Pharisaic Judaism, the ancestor of all modern Judaism, spread.

Jewish communities of the Mediterranean world

In the other parts of the Mediterranean world the Jews did not suffer from the persecution of the Syrian king Antiochus, and continued to develop in peace. In many cities by the time of Jesus there were large and flourishing Jewish communities. In Egyptian Alexandria they obtained the right to function as a political entity within the state, a city within a city, with its own administration. Cyrene in North Africa was not dissimilar. But in many cities inscriptions show that there were synagogues; and large cities like Corinth or Rome had many synagogues, and therefore many different Jewish communities. Each of these communities was ruled by a council of elders (in Greek *presbyteroi*, whence our 'presbyters'), presided by an *archisynagogos* ('president of the synagogue'). This was a temporary and elective office, which could be held several times by the same man.

Most societies dislike strangers, especially if the societies are clannish and rich. The Jews were forced by their peculiarities and their differences from others (and especially their idea of cultic purity) to keep themselves to themselves and clear of others. Others did not really understand them and their strange ways, and consequently were suspicious of them. The Jews trusted each other; they could by Law charge each other no interest on loans, and this had helped them to become already a comparatively rich group. They also had a somewhat special relationship with the Roman emperors: their unpopularity made them rely on the emperor for protection, and the emperor normally took advantage of this to use them as supporters in the various cities. This in turn made them more unpopular.

The Pax Romana

By the time of the New Testament, communication between these communities was frequent and easy. The whole Mediterranean world was ruled by Rome. But Rome, once it had conquered the world, did little more than ensure that the peace was kept, that there was a reasonable amount of justice, and that Rome made enough money out of the provincials not only to pay for its armies but also to ensure a lavish income for its officials who administered them. The Romans had a stranglehold over most financial transactions within the empire. But the whole area was a network of independent city-states, each with its own constitution and system of government, often ruling only a few hundred square kilometres of territory. This system was practicable because Rome prevented armed squabbles between these little states, and would judge cases of dispute between them. The Romans realised that local rulers understand their own people best, and also spared themselves the trouble of administering these territories, apart from taxing them interest – interest which these rulers of course recouped from their subjects. Taxation was doubtless heavy, but modern estimates vary about just how oppressive it was to the poorer people.

Travel was easy because of the Pax Romana, the Roman peace which prevailed everywhere from 31 BC for a couple of centuries. Roman rule ensured that there was no war and no piracy. The great Roman roads, like 4-metre-wide walls sunk into the ground, crisscrossed the Roman world. This made land traffic easier and more rapid than it would be for another 1800 years. In crisis the emperor Tiberius once rode 300 kilometres (with frequent changes of horses) in 24 hours. A steady 15–25 kilometres a day was uncomfortable and tiring but possible for the ordinary traveller by road. By sea travel was far quicker, though kept to an essential minimum in the dangerous winter – losses at sea were frequent; a high proportion of the legal cases which have come down to us concern insurance disputes. Rome to Alexandria was possible in five days by ship, and Scipio demonstrated to the Roman senate how dangerously close Africa was to Italy by showing them a fig picked in Carthage the previous day. Trade flourished, and one merchant in Asia Minor claims on his tombstone to have made over seventy journeys to Rome. It has been calculated that in his dozen years of journeying Paul covered over 15,000 kilometres – and he was settled in Corinth or Ephesus for several of those years.

In this unified world there were travelling preachers and teachers in large numbers. Students travelled to different universities from Rome, but especially to Athens. Philosophers of the school called 'Cynics' travelled in poverty to spread their brand of knowledge. Those with means and leisure travelled to the famous shrines and centres of healing, like the shrine of Aesculapius at Epidaurus in Greece, whence stem a number of tales of miraculous healing. There were special centres of the 'mystery religions', promising salvation to those who were initiated into their secret rites, whose secrets were so closely guarded that they were never written down and have remained largely secret to this day. Among these hordes of religious travellers and pilgrims, people like Paul and his companions, peddling their own particular recipe for salvation, would have excited little comment. The scene in the Acts of the Apostles of Paul being invited to speak to a group of philosophers at Athens is true to life. It was this ease of travel which enabled Paul to make his missionary journeys, travelling between the Jewish communities in Asia Minor and Greece, and to send the letters which have come down to us. His letters also provide evidence of the frequency of travel and communication between other members of these communities. The greetings at the end of the Letter to the Romans especially show how many people in the Christian community at Rome Paul had met, and how many more he knew about, even without going to Rome.

2 THE TRADITION BEHIND THE GOSPELS

The literary character of the gospels as we have them leaves no doubt that the gospel material was handed down for some years by word of mouth. Education in the ancient world included a large measure of memorisation, since books were scarce and expensive. In the Jewish schools of the first century pupils learnt the Bible by heart, and then went on to learn by heart the sayings of the rabbis. With memories so trained, learning the tradition of the deeds and sayings of Jesus would pose no problem to the first Christians. Passages learnt by heart are preserved for us in the letters of Paul.

The early *kerygma*

Two passages in the First Letter to the Corinthians clearly formed part of the basic instruction in Christianity learnt by heart by the new converts.

Paul writes:

> The tradition I handed on to you in the first place, a tradition which I had myself received, was that **Christ died for our sins,**

in accordance with the scriptures, and that he was buried; and that on the third day he was raised to life, in accordance with the scriptures; and that he appeared to Cephas; and later to the Twelve; and next he appeared to more than five hundred of the brothers at the same time (1 Co 15:3–5)

This statement was not coined by Paul himself. The words for 'handed on' and 'received' are the technical terms used in rabbinic literature for the passing on and learning by heart of the traditions of the elders. Various terms used in the statement itself are uncharacteristic of Paul. He always speaks of 'sin' in the singular, not the plural as here. He never uses the expression 'the Twelve', and so on. This passage therefore represents the basic statement of the Resurrection, learnt by heart by new converts.

Similarly about the eucharist he writes:

For the tradition I received from the Lord and also handed on to you is that **on the night he was betrayed, the Lord Jesus took some bread, and after he had given thanks, he broke it, and he said, 'This is my body, which is for you; do this in remembrance of me.' And in the same way, with the cup after supper, saying, 'This cup is the new covenant in my blood. Whenever you drink it, do this as a memorial of me.'** (1 Co 11:23–5)

Again he introduces the statement by the same technical terms, and again there are expressions uncharacteristic of Paul. Elsewhere he uses 'body' only of the Christian community. Several uncharacteristic grammatical constructions are apparent in the Greek text, though not in the English. This statement on the eucharist differs from the account in the gospels only in minute particulars. It is probably a different form of the same tradition, handed down to all new Christians and eventually incorporated into the gospel text.

Christian hymns

The first Christians were encouraged to bring their own hymns to the liturgical assembly. Paul writes, 'When you come together each of you brings a psalm or some instruction or a revelation' (I Corinthians 14:26). From the letters of Pliny, the Roman governor of Bithynia half a century later, we know that the Christians came together, as he put it, 'to sing hymns to Christ as to a god' (Epistles, Book 10, letter 96).

One such hymn may have been used by Paul in Philippians 2:6–11 (the following text is my own translation):

> **being in the form of God,**
> **he did not count equality with God**
> **something to be grasped.**
>
> **But he emptied himself,**
> **taking the form of a Servant,**
> **becoming as human beings are;**
> **and being in every way like a human being,**
> **he was humbler yet,**
> **even to accepting death**, death on a cross.
>
> **And for this God raised him high,**
> **and gave him the name which is above all other names;**
>
> **so that at the name of Jesus every knee should bend**
>   in the heavens, on earth and in the underworld,
> **and every tongue acknowledge Jesus Christ as Lord**
>   to the glory of God the Father.

Paul's additions (according to one reconstruction – the details are disputed) are given in normal type. In this hymn there are at least four expressions never otherwise used by Paul, as well as other differences. For example, Paul himself applies the word and the theology of the Servant of the Lord to himself, not to Christ. The carefully balanced structure is also quite unlike Paul's nervous and staccato way of writing. This is probably, therefore, another piece of traditional material incorporated into the New Testament.

3 THE ORAL TRADITION OF THE GOSPELS

The variety of the tradition

The variety of forms in which a single saying on the same matter has come down to us shows that the sayings circulated in different forms.

Sayings on divorce

Paul's version of Jesus' saying on divorce differs from those in the gospels, in a way which is compatible only with being handed down orally:

> To the married I give this ruling, and this is not mine but the Lord's: a wife must not be separated from her husband – or if she has already left him, she must remain unmarried or else be reconciled to her husband – and a husband must not divorce his wife.
> (1 Co 7:10–11)

> Whoever divorces his wife and marries another is guilty of adultery against her. And if a woman divorces her husband and marries another she is guilty of adultery too.   (Mk 10:11–12)

> everyone who divorces his wife, except for the case of an illicit marriage, makes her an adulteress; and anyone who marries a divorced woman commits adultery.   (Mt 5:32)

Sayings on the reward due to missioners

Similarly Paul's saying on the reward due to a missioner is probably based on the name saying as Matthew 10:10 and Luke 10.7:

> the labourer deserves his keep.   (Mt 10:10)

> those who preach the gospel should get their living from the gospel.   (1 Co 9:14)

Contemporary stories of miracles

Eusebius (*Historia Ecclesiastica* 3:39:8–9) quotes from Papias, Bishop of Hierapolis at the beginning of the second century, traditions of miracles not contained in the gospels or the Acts: one a tradition of raising of the dead, passed down by the daughters of Philip; and another that Justus Barsabas drank poison without being harmed. These may be examples only of stories circulating in the Christian community which were not finally included in the gospels. At some stage there must have been a selection process. Some scholars would hold that the so-called

Gospel of Thomas contains many sayings which represent a different oral tradition of sayings contained in the canonical gospels.

The synoptic gospels and John's gospel

The relationship between the three synoptic gospels will be considered later, but it is clear that the same story or saying is often contained in the Gospel of John in a different form from that given in the synoptics. The story of the Healing at Cana in John 4:46–53 is similar in many but not all respects to that given in Matthew 8:5–13 and Luke 7:1–10; the kind of similarity and difference can best be explained in terms of oral tradition. Similarly the Anointing at Bethany in Mark 14:3–9 and Matthew 26:6–13 is probably an oral tradition of the same story as that given in John 12:1–8. A third example is the synoptic account of the Agony in the Garden and the Johannine sayings about the approaching Passion in John 12:27: 'Now my soul is troubled. What shall I say, Father, save me from this hour? But it is for this very reason that I have come to this hour.'

A number of sayings in John could be from the same oral tradition as those in the synoptics:

I am not fit to undo the strap of his sandal.   (Jn 1:27)

I am not fit to carry his sandals   (Mt 3:11)

Anyone who loves his life loses it; anyone who hates his life in this world will keep it for eternal life.   (Jn 12:25)

anyone who loses his life for my sake, and for the sake of the gospel, will save it.   (Mk 8:35)

If you forgive anyone's sins, they are forgiven; if you retain anyone's sins, they are retained.   (Jn 20:23)

Whatever you bind on earth will be bound in heaven; whatever you loose on earth will be loosed in heaven.   (Mt 18:18)

whoever welcomes the one I send, welcomes me, and whoever welcomes me, welcomes the one who sent me.   (Jn 13:20)

Anyone who welcomes you welcomes me; and anyone who welcomes me welcomes the one who sent me.   (Mt 10:40)

'Pearls on a string'

In the years after the First World War three German scholars were responsible for the development of the method known as the 'history of forms' or 'form criticism' (*Formgeschichte*). Karl Ludwig Schmidt, Martin Dibelius and Rudolf Bultmann started from the assumption that the gospels were handed down orally, not as one entity but as units which were subsequently joined together 'like pearls on a string'. Single units, stories or sayings, were originally independent, and their framework is purely conventional. Typically in Mark this framework consists of such expressions as 'and immediately', 'again', 'and he said to them'. For the purpose of classification, one list of these units is as follows.

Sayings

1. *Logia* These are classified into five groups.
    (a) Wisdom sayings: e.g. 'The Sabbath was made for man, not man for the Sabbath' (Mk 2:27).
    (b) Eschatological sayings: e.g. 'if anyone . . . is ashamed of me and of my words, the Son of man will also be ashamed of him when he comes in the glory of his Father with the holy angels' (Mk 8:38).
    (c) Disciplinary sayings: e.g. 'the time will come when the bridegroom is taken away from them, and then, on that day, they will fast' (Mk 2:20).
    (d) I-sayings: e.g. 'the Son of man is master even of the Sabbath' (Mk 2:28)
    (e) Parables: either stories, e.g. the Sower (Mk 4:3–8); or simple images, e.g. new wine in new wineskins (Mk 2:22).

2. *Apophthegms or pronouncement stories* (more recently called by the Greek work 'chreiai') These are stories centred upon a pronouncement of Jesus. They are classified into two groups.
    (a) Controversies: e.g. the story of the Forgiveness of Sins (Mk 2:5–10).
    (b) Instructional stories: e.g. the story of the True Kinsmen of Jesus (Mk 3:31–5).

Stories

1. *Miracle stories* Again, there are two groups.
    (a) Healing stories: e.g. the Cure of a Leper (Mk 1:40–5).
    (b) Nature miracles: e.g. the Calming of the Storm (Mk 4:35–41).

2. *Historical stories and legends* These include the Baptism, the Temptations, and the Transfiguration. (The difference between historical stories and legends lies in their relationship to a historical content. According to Dibelius, legends 'have no special interest in history . . .

in the modern sense they are not historical accounts at all'. All three original proponents of form criticism had minimal interest in the historicity of the gospels. Their Lutheran emphasis was on the encounter with Christ in the present, to which the historical Christ was almost an obstacle. For example, Dibelius held that history which can be identified by the historico-critical method is 'world'; consequently God is not to be found in it. Similarly Bultmann held that what is known cannot be the object of faith: if a story has historical content it is outside the realm of faith. It is not by any means necessary, however, to deny that the accounts of the Baptism, the Temptations and the Transfiguration have a basis in fact: merely a different genre or type of writing is used – for example, plentiful scriptural allusion – from that used by modern historians. It is not unexpected that popular writers of twenty centuries ago used different conventions from those of the present day.)

The purpose of this classification was to compare and contrast the units of the gospel with similar stories in the folk literature of the time. It also helps to isolate the most important elements in each unit and to understand better the formation and purpose of the stories. A subsequent important step was to deduce the circumstances in which a story might have been told. For example, the disciplinary saying about fasting quoted above might well have been passed down in the context of discussions (either within the Christian community or with outsiders) about whether Christians should obey Pharisaic legislation concerning regular fasts.

4 TOWARDS A WRITTEN GOSPEL

Between the stage of these individual units of gospel tradition and the first written gospel there may have been an intermediary stage. This would have been represented by two factors: the outline of the *kerygma* and partial collections.

The outline of the *kerygma*

C. H. Dodd pointed out in *The Apostolic Preaching and its Developments* (1963) that all the initial proclamations about Jesus made by Peter and Paul in the Acts of the Apostles have the same basic pattern, best seen in Peter's speech to Cornelius:

You know what happened all over Judaea, how Jesus of Nazareth
began in Galilee, after John had been preaching baptism. God had
anointed him with the Holy Spirit and with power, and because
God was with him, Jesus went about doing good and curing all
who had fallen into the power of the devil. Now we are witnesses
to everything he did throughout the countryside of Judaea and in
Jerusalem itself: and they killed him by hanging him on a tree, yet
on the third day God raised him to life and allowed him to be
seen   (Ac 10:37–40)

This contains in order the elements of all synoptic gospels:

> Beginning in Galilee:
>   preaching of the Baptist;
>   Baptism/Anointing of Jesus;
>   doing good and curing;
>   apostolic witnesses.
> In Judaea and Jerusalem:
>   Crucifixion;
>   Resurrection.

The basic outline of the synoptic gospels accords, therefore, with the
original preaching of the apostles.

Partial collections

Before the actual collections of the gospels there may have existed
smaller and partial collections of material, which predated and were
used by the evangelists. Larger units which have been suggested included
these:

1. *Mark 1:21–38 – the Day at Capernaum* A series of four incidents
   which together make up a sample day of Jesus' activity in Capernaum, immediately after the call of the first disciples.

2. *Mark 2:1—3:6 – Early Controversies* A series of five controversies
   with the Pharisees, which climax in the Pharisees' plot to destroy
   Jesus.

3. *Mark 6:30—8:21 – the Bread Section* A series of incidents, beginning
   with the first Multiplication of Loaves, and ending with the second
   Multiplication of Loaves and the reflection on them. All the incidents
   have some connection with bread or eating. It is suggested further

(less probably, I think) that this could originally have been a eucharistic instruction.

4. *Mark 12:13–37 – Four Controversies* In the first three Jesus is questioned by representatives of the major parties of the Jews; in the fourth he takes the initiative by questioning them himself.

5. *Mark 14:1—16:8 – The narrative of the Passion, Death and Resurrection of Jesus* This is often held to have been the first long continuous narrative, and to be extremely ancient.

Whether these are considered to be pre-existing collections or units within the gospel assembled by the evangelist himself depends on a view of the originality, style and method of the first evangelist. This has yet to be investigated.

5 BIBLIOGRAPHY

For the sociological background, and (particularly Brown and Meier) for studies of individual Christian communities:

Brown, Raymond E., *The Churches the Apostles Left Behind Them*, London, Geoffrey Chapman, 1984.

Brown, Raymond E., and Meier, John P., *Antioch and Rome*, London, Geoffrey Chapman, 1983.

Meeks, Wayne A., *The First Urban Christians: the social world of the apostle Paul*, Yale, Yale University Press, 1983.

O'Connor, Jerome Murphy, *St Paul's Corinth: text and archaeology*, Wilmington, Michael Glazier, 1983.

Sherwin-White, A. N. *Roman Society and Roman Law in the New Testament*, Oxford, Clarendon Press, 1963.

For oral tradition as shown in the relationship between John and the synoptics:

Dodd, C. H., 'Four Johannine *Herrenworte*', *New Testament Studies*, **2** (1955), 75–86.

Dunn, James D. G., 'John and the oral gospel tradition', in Henry Wansbrough (ed.), *Jesus and the Oral Gospel Tradition*, Sheffield, Sheffield Academic Press, 1991.

For the theory of form criticism:

Bultmann, Rudolf, *History of the Synoptic Tradition* (tr. John Marsh), Oxford, Blackwell, 1963.

Dibelius, Martin, *From Tradition to Gospel* (tr. Bertram Lee Wilson), London, Nicholson & Watson, 1934.

Sanders, E. P. and Davies, Margaret, *Studying the Synoptic Gospels* Part III, London, SCM, 1989.

For the pattern of the apostolic preaching:

Dodd, C. H., *The Apostolic Preaching and its Developments*, London, Hodder & Stoughton, 1936.

6 PERSONAL STUDY

1. Find for yourself in Mark one of each of the ten types of literary units described on pages 13–14.
2. Read Paul's letter to Philemon and write Philemon's reply to Paul. Philemon would want to include many details of his life and circumstances as a Hellenistic Christian surrounded by both Hellenistic non-believers and Christians converted from Judaism.

CHAPTER 2

MARK – THE FIRST GOSPEL?

1 THE PROBLEM

The first three gospels share so much material that there must be a literary relationship between them. The same pattern of events is visible in each of them (with some alterations) – this is why they were given the name 'synoptic' gospels ('synoptic' means 'at one glance'); the three gospels can be set out in parallel columns in a synopsis, to show the relationships. Only two incidents of Mark are wholly missing from Matthew and Luke. In some incidents their language is identical for long stretches.

These similarities cannot be coincidental. For the last two hundred years it has been hotly debated whether Mark or Matthew is the basis used by the others. Alternatively it has been suggested that both of them, and also Luke, depend on an earlier written version of the gospel, or even on several slightly different versions.

It is important for several reasons to establish which of the gospels was written first. Firstly, historically, it is valuable to know the most primitive and original form of the tradition: here we are closest to the original words of Jesus. Secondly, it is important theologically, as the evangelists edit and adapt the material to express their own and their Church's view of Christ and the Church. For instance, by selection of material and by little touches and alterations here and there, Matthew stresses the dignity and majesty of Jesus more than does Mark. He also pays closer attention to the Christian community and its problems and leadership. Luke, for his part, concentrates more on the themes such as the loving forgiveness of God, the need for prayer, and the danger of wealth. Mark's gospel is simpler and fresher, concentrating on the revelation of the person of Jesus and the wonder of it. As each of the evangelists has such different emphases and points of view, it is important to see the line of development. In this way it is easier to understand the exact emphases of the theology of the evangelists.

Views on the priority of a particular gospel and of the origin of the others are strongly held. It may not be possible to reach a firm and final conclusion, but in any consideration of the gospels it is important to have at least a working hypothesis on the matter as a basis of consideration.

2 THE EXTERNAL EVIDENCE

The external evidence about the writing of the gospels stems from Papias, bishop of Hierapolis in the early second century. He is quoted by Eusebius, the Church historian, some two hundred years later; but Eusebius, who knew considerably more of his writings than we do, did not value his evidence highly. In any case the meaning of almost every phrase of his statement has been disputed. In practice scholars who quote Papias do so very selectively, quoting simply those parts of his statement which agree with their already-formed theory, and rejecting the rest. We will therefore not consider the evidence of Papias, but investigate the evidence of the gospels themselves.

3 THE TWO-DOCUMENT THEORY

The most widely-held theory is the two-document theory. During most of the present century this view has reigned supreme, and in most circles it is still simply taken for granted. For instance, in the authoritative *New Jerome Biblical Commentary*, in the article on the Synoptic Problem (no. 40), Frans Neirynck, one of the most dedicated and dauntingly learned of its proponents, gives fourteen columns to the exposition of this theory, and only two to 'alternative solutions'.

The theory

Mark was the first of the three synoptic gospels to be written. If all three evangelists relate a saying or an incident, Mark is the source used by Matthew and Luke. If Mark has no account of a saying or incident but Matthew and Luke have an account at least broadly similar to each other's, they both rely on a collection of Sayings of the Lord. This collection, which is called Q, no longer exists; it disappeared at an early date, and is merely deduced from the accounts. It is likely to have been a collection merely of Sayings, because the similarity between Matthew and Luke, unsupported by Mark, occurs only in passages which are sayings, not incidents.

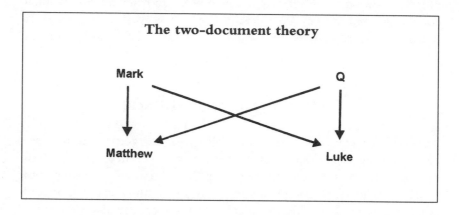

The two-document theory

Mark   Q

Matthew   Luke

Arguments in favour

1. *The order* In the vast majority of instances the material which all three evangelists share occurs in Matthew and Luke in the same order of units as it does in Mark. Where the order does differ, it can be explained in terms of the theological interests or other editorial tendencies typical of the evangelist. For instance, Matthew is a careful teacher, and gathers Sayings into great collections. This leads him sometimes to give Markan material earlier in the sequence than does Mark himself. Thus for the first great collection of Sayings, the Sermon on the Mount, Matthew uses teaching which occurs only later in Mark (e.g. the prohibition of divorce). Similarly, for his great collection of miracles in Chapters 8—9 he uses stories (e.g. the Calming of the Storm) which occur only later in Mark.

2. *Detailed editing* Both the language and the theology of Matthew and Luke are more developed than those of Mark. Repeatedly Matthew and Luke iron out the roughnesses of Mark's primitive Greek. They also, with little touches and omissions, present a more dignified picture of Jesus, expressing more clearly his majesty and glory. They show greater reverence for the disciples, omitting much of Jesus' criticism of their slowness to understand, which is a major feature in Mark.

It is possible that Mark deliberately roughened the more sophisticated Greek which he found in his sources, but it is not likely. It is possible that he wished to present a less exalted picture of Jesus, making him more attractively human. It is also possible that he himself inserted the criticisms of the disciples in order to show that Jesus' own followers were no less slow to believe than later followers. These things are possible — but none is likely.

Difficulties

1. *It is difficult to form a coherent picture of Q* Closer examination shows a number of passages given by all three evangelists in which Matthew and Luke show such similarity to each other over against Mark that protagonists of this theory have to resort to the claim that the passage was present both in Mark and in Q. Q therefore grows beyond the limits of a Sayings-Source, used to supplement Mark. For some of these incidents (e.g. the Temptations) it can be argued that these are basically Sayings material with a minimal narrative framework. For others (e.g. the Cure of a Leper in Mark 1:40–5) this cannot be said. It must therefore be admitted that Q cannot have been simply a collection of Sayings with an occasional narrative framework.

2. *In many passages Matthew and Luke agree against Mark* This occurs so frequently that it is difficult to attribute the agreements to chance or to independent editing. Even granted that they each wanted to change Mark, it becomes overwhelmingly coincidental that they should independently have reached exactly the same conclusion again and again. If Matthew knew Luke or Luke knew Matthew, there is no need to posit Q at all. Matthew could have used Luke directly, or vice versa.

4 THE TWO-GOSPEL HYPOTHESIS

This hypothesis was first fully argued by J. J. Griesbach in 1789, and is often called 'the Griesbach hypothesis'. It has been revived in the last thirty years, and now enjoys a certain amount of support.

The hypothesis

Matthew was the first gospel to be written, for Christians of Jewish origin. Luke was written next, sometime before AD 60, for Paul's gentile converts. The two were combined by Mark, who selected sometimes from Matthew, sometimes from Luke, zigzagging from one to the other between incidents, and sometimes within incidents.

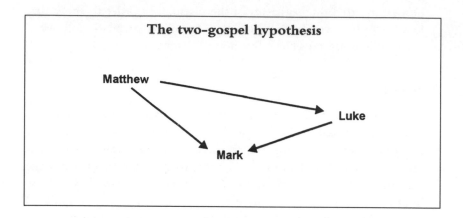

The two-gospel hypothesis

Matthew

Luke

Mark

Arguments in favour

1. *Double expressions* Frequently Mark has a double expression (1:32: 'That evening, after sunset') of which one half occurs in Matthew (8:16: 'That evening) and the other in Luke (4:40: 'At sunset'). This occurs, it is argued, too frequently for it to be explained by the coincidence that Matthew and Luke happened to choose different halves of the Markan expression; more economical is the solution that Mark chose both Matthew's and Luke's versions.

2. *The order* The order of material in Mark may be explained on the supposition that it was composed from Matthew and Luke. Mark zigzags from Matthew to Luke and back again, without ever turning back on their order. Sometimes his order is supported by both of them, but always by one or the other.

3. *Tradition* 'The priority of Matthew went unchallenged by orthodox or heretic for the best part of two thousand years'.[1] This is perhaps an overstatement of the evidence, but from Irenaeus in the late second century onwards many Church fathers held that Matthew was the first gospel to be written. Irenaeus himself said that Matthew wrote while Peter and Paul were still evangelising Rome, and Mark only 'after their death'.

[1] Bernard Orchard, *Downside Review* 106 (1988), p. 104.

Difficulties

1. *There are omissions* It is difficult to see why Mark should have discarded so much of Matthew's and Luke's material, the Infancy Stories, the great discourses of Matthew (at least partly echoed in Luke), the appearances of the Risen Lord, and much else. It is hard to see also why he should have composed an account both linguistically and theologically so much more primitive than those of his models.

2. *The order is inconclusive* The argument from the 'zigzagging' order is valid only if Mark is first established on other grounds to be dependent on Matthew and Luke. It is also possible to make sense of the order of Matthew and Luke on the supposition that Mark is the first gospel.

3. *The evidence is questionable* The patristic evidence is not so one-sided as has been represented. Nor is it clear that Irenaeus, who stands at its head, really knew what he was talking about, a full century after the composition of the gospels. Some of his wording suggests that he was interpreting Papias, who states no such thing.

5 THE 'MULTIPLE ATTESTATION' THEORY

This theory, extremely detailed and complicated, is associated with the name of M.-E. Boismard and other distinguished scholars of the French Dominican *École biblique* in Jerusalem. It has received little attention from the non-Francophone scholarly community, perhaps partly because of its complications. Each incident and saying has to be taken for itself, and one of its most profound tenets is that any simplistic, overall solution fails to take account of all the evidence.

The theory

The gospel tradition stems basically from three documents: A (a Palestinian proto-gospel), B (a gentile-Christian revision of A) and C (a third document of varied character, which acts as a wild card in the theory). Each of the gospels which we now have has passed through several stages of editing, with crisscrossing influences from other intermediate stages of other gospels. For instance, the final version of Mark has details which show that it was influenced by the final version of Luke. The narrative framework of Mark is at the base of all three gospels, and in its turn depends on a previous version, named by Boismard 'intermediate Mark'. The full history of the texts can be discovered only with the use of patristic quotations, which often show minute variations from the present gospel texts, reflecting earlier versions of the gospels.

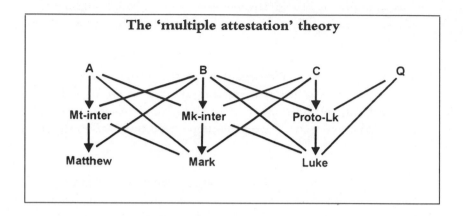

The 'multiple attestation' theory

Arguments in favour

1. *A and B are plausible* A coherent picture and a clear characterisation are presented of at least the two documents A and B, which are taken to be at the base of the tradition.

2. *The relationships between the gospel texts* The argumentation for the development of each passage is so detailed that it defies any attempt to summarise it or to generalise. The 'crisscrossing' is founded on the fact that expressions which seem characteristic of one gospel are found in another, and may be attributed to the influence of each gospel on each other at a late stage of the evolution of the tradition.

3. *Simpler theories are inadequate* Even if the detailed conclusions of Boismard are not exactly accepted, the very fact of the continuance of the debate outlined above shows that there are phenomena which do not fit any of the simpler theories.

Difficulties

1. *Textual features may predate the written texts* The process described may well apply to the development of the oral tradition before the gospel material came to be written down. Such crisscrossing and interaction

would fit the more fluid consistency of a body of oral tradition, passing backwards and forwards between many witnesses, better than they fit more defined and fixed written sources.

2. *The theory presumes a 'tidy' development* The detective work involved in this theory presupposes that each of the characters involved in the plot behaved with inflexible predictability and consistency. The theory is too logical and too conjectural for a literary process.

3. *Differences may result from misremembering* The variations in the quotations in early Church Fathers may reflect their own faulty memories rather than differences in the original texts.

6 THE SINGLE-SOURCE THEORY

Recently an attractive theory has been gaining ground, promoted by M. D. Goulder, based on Markan priority without the Sayings-Source Q. This is a revival and extension of the position of the Oxford scholar, Austin Farrer, 'On Dispensing with Q'.[2]

The theory

Matthew's only written source was Mark, which he edited and developed through his own resources. The material in Matthew which is not drawn from Mark, and the treatment of the Markan material, shows a consistency of method and approach which can only be the indication of one mind. The elements said to be characteristic of Q are in fact characteristic of Matthew, since they appear also in the passages peculiar to Matthew and in his editing of Mark. Many of these elaborations are developed from reflection on the life and meaning of Jesus in the light of the scriptures, by methods reminiscent of contemporary Jewish exegesis, known as 'midrash'. Similarly Luke results from a stylistically and theologically consistent editing of Matthew and Mark, without any need to postulate a further written source. There is therefore no need to postulate any written source for the synoptic gospels other than Mark.

[2] In D. E. Nineham (ed.), *Studies in the Gospels* (Oxford, Blackwell, 1955).

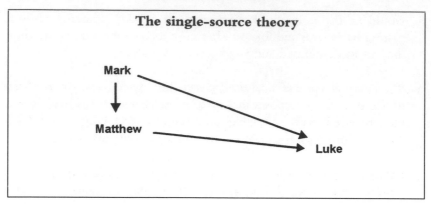

The single-source theory

Mark

Matthew

Luke

Arguments in favour

1. *The detail is persuasive* The detailed arguments for the homogeneity of Matthean style and interests are presented with forceful detail in M. Goulder's *Midrash and Lection in Matthew* (SPCK, 1976), and for Luke in his *Luke – A New Paradigm* (Sheffield Academic Press, 1989). Without giving a detailed résumé one can only say that they are careful and convincing.

2. *The theory deals with the links between Matthew and Luke* This theory accounts for the multiplicity of the so-called 'minor agreements' of Matthew with Luke, which despite attempted explanations remains a problem for the two-document theory.

Difficulties

1. *The process seems unlikely* Such an explanation of Luke must postulate that Luke worked with both Matthew's and Mark's gospels spread out before him, carefully collating the two and studiously moving from one to the other with detailed editing. Is this not more probable for a modern collator than for an ancient author?

2. *Some variations are surprising* Much of Matthew's great discourses (such as the Sermon on the Mount) appears in shorter passages in Luke: is it probable that Luke should so have broken up these carefully crafted discourses? Goulder holds that Luke's motive was to break them into manageable units which could be more easily assimilated.

3. *An earlier source might be expected* Is it really acceptable that the evangelists should themselves have so extensively developed the gospel tradition without any historical basis, or at least without any further detailed historical data?

7 CONCLUSION

There is no easy and generally accepted solution to the Synoptic Problem. Each of the above positions is held by responsible scholars, arguing with fervour and conviction. None is without its difficulties.

I myself am convinced of the priority of Mark, and incline towards the last solution outlined. For this reason the priority of Mark will be the working hypothesis of this book.

8 BIBLIOGRAPHY

This chapter is a slightly altered version of an article which originally appeared in *Priests and People* 5 (1991), pp. 265–9.

Apart from the works referred to above, a short discussion is given in most introductions to the New Testament or the gospels, e.g. Graham N. Stanton, *The Gospels and Jesus* (Oxford, Oxford University Press, 1989), pp. 35–9.

A thorough and balanced discussion, with examples, may be found in E. P. Sanders and Margaret Davies, *Studying the Synoptic Gospels* (London, SCM, 1989), pp. 51–119.

9 PERSONAL STUDY

1. Prepare your tools. Make your own 'synopsis' of the unit about Jesus' baptism: Matthew 3:13–17; Mark 1:9–11; Luke 3:21–2. Put the texts side by side. (The most convenient way may be to photocopy each of the three versions.) The texts must be:
(a) either the Greek texts or literal translations – the most suitable versions are probably the RSV, NRSV or NJB;
(b) texts you can scribble on;
(c) three texts which you have under your eye at the same time.

Prepare either highlighters or crayons of three colours, e.g. red, blue and green.

2. Colour in *boldly* words shared by Mark and Matthew in colour 1, words shared by Mark and Luke in colour 2, words shared by Matthew and Luke in colour 3. (Some words, common to all three evangelists, will end up double-coloured.)

3. You can then do the following.

(a) Note what is special in each evangelist's account. For example, in Matthew 3:17 the voice addresses the crowds about Jesus; in Luke what part does John the Baptist play? Is the baptism Luke's main interest?

(b) Make a *preliminary* assessment about which theory fits this unit best. Note the minor agreements between Matthew and Luke. Both of them have the heavens 'open', a word which does not occur in Mark. Another minor agreement probably disappears in translation; the Greek has one word for 'on him' in both Matthew and Luke, and a different word in Mark. If you find this frustrating and have a wee bit of spare time, learn Greek.

PART II

Mark: the earliest gospel

CHAPTER 3

HOW DID MARK SET ABOUT WRITING HIS GOSPEL?

1 THE NOTION OF A GOSPEL

It is clear already that Mark did not receive from the tradition more than a very general outline of Jesus' ministry as a framework for arranging the incidents and sayings received from the tradition. It is, in any case, a mistake to assume that an ancient biography must follow the rules of a modern biography, which normally proceeds chronologically. Plutarch's *Lives*, written a half-century or so later than Mark, begin with the births and youth of his characters and end with their deaths; but apart from that basic framework, the *Lives* group the incidents and anecdotes by quite different principles. Mark's purpose was not merely to relate the life of his hero but to pass on his message of the Good News.

The Greek work for 'gospel' (εὐαῦγέλιον) came only subsequently to be used for a book of the gospels. It was already used frequently by Paul for the message which he brought. It is a favourite word of his; sixty of the seventy-six uses of the noun in the New Testament come in his letters; of the other instances half come in Mark. Luke never uses the noun but frequently uses the verb, 'to preach the gospel', which he alone of the gospel-writers uses. Paul seems to use the concept chiefly to distinguish his message of Good News from the Jewish way of salvation based on the Law. As with many of Paul's concepts, it is disputed whether he derived this idea from Hellenistic or from Jewish sources. In the Hellenistic world the expression is associated chiefly with the cult of the Roman emperor. It was used to describe the good

news of the crowning of an emperor, or a victory by him, or the birth
of an heir, or even the news that he was to make a state visit to the
city. Since the emperor was regarded as a god, such events had
the overtones of the manifestation of a god to his people, a moment of
joy and celebration. But it is also possible that Paul was following Jesus'
own usage of the term. It certainly comes in a passage of Isaiah which
seems to have been formative in his thought (61:1; compare Matthew
11:2–6):

> The spirit of Lord Yahweh is on me,
> for Yahweh has anointed me.
> He has sent me to bring the [good] news to the afflicted,
> to soothe the broken-hearted, . . .

But it is not clear that any of its uses in Mark reflects a saying of Jesus.

The authentic words of Jesus

In view of the process through which the gospel material passed, it
cannot be simply assumed that any one of the sayings on the lips of
Jesus in the gospels was actually spoken by him. The material was passed
down in particular situations, and was used and applied or adapted to
those situations. The form-critical school, with its extreme anti-histori-
cal bias, was very ready to assume that sayings were simply created in
the name of the Risen Lord to provide answers to and guidance
about the problems facing the early Christians. They point out, for
instance, that the controversy at Antioch between Paul and the supporters of James over eating ritually unclean food (reported in Galatians
2:11–14) and the debate at Jerusalem, which led to the decisions of Acts
15:29, could scarcely have occurred if Jesus had already solved the
problem as he appears to do in Mark 7:18–19, declaring all foods clean.
It would have been strange if Paul had not solved the problem once
and for all by quoting this scene, if it had already been known.

Criteria have therefore been evolved by which to judge whether a
saying can safely be considered to stem from Jesus himself. The most
important of these are:

1. *Criterion of embarrassment* A scene would be unlikely to have been
    invented by the early Church if it was theologically embarrassing.
    Examples: the death of Jesus as a despised criminal; the baptism of
    Jesus the Messiah by his inferior, John (the embarrassment is evident
    in Matthew's account); Jesus' ignorance of the Day of the Lord (Mk
    13:32); and the betrayal of Jesus by Peter and the other 'followers' at
    the time of the Passion.

2. *Criterion of discontinuity* If a teaching was radically different from contemporary teaching in Judaism (e.g. the idea of a suffering Messiah does not appear in first century Judaism) and was not used by the early Church (e.g. the idea of Jesus as the Suffering Servant of the Lord is hardly used in Paul or Acts), it reflects Jesus' own mind. The difficulty about this is that it excludes too much. In general, Jesus' teaching was in continuity with the teaching of Judaism, and one would expect it to be followed by the early Church! It is odd that the concept of Jesus as the Suffering Servant hardly appears in the Church's reflection on Jesus.

3. *Criterion of multiple attestation* If a saying or scene appears in several sources, especially in slightly different forms, then this too is likely to come from Jesus himself. Examples: the miraculous Feeding of the Multitude (one of the few miracles which occurs in John as well as in the synoptics, and in two different forms in Mark); and the sayings on service, that those who lose their lives will save them (Mk 8:35; Mt 10:39; Jn 12:25).

4. *Criterion of rejection* The final outcome of Jesus' ministry was indubitably his rejection and execution. Events which lead up to this are logical preliminaries. Examples: the 'cleansing' of the Temple; the clash with the Jewish authorities.

Less reliable, but also quite useful, indications are these:

5. *Sayings that bear traces of translation from Aramaic* These must date from the earliest times, for Christianity soon moved out of the Aramaic-speaking sphere into the Greek world. The expression 'Son of Man' is uncouth in Greek, but perfectly natural in Aramaic. But of course Jesus was not the only Aramaic-speaking prophetic figure around.

6. *Sayings that betray the countryman's eye* (e.g. the mustard seed, 'foxes have holes') This sharpness of eye and use of country imagery seem to have been characteristic of Jesus, and Christianity early moved principally into the cities. But there were other observant prophets about, and foxes are often seen in Wimbledon and Manchester.

These criteria may be used to guarantee as authentic some sayings and deeds of Jesus. It must be remembered, however, that they are harshly exclusive: there must be other authentic sayings of Jesus which do not fall into these categories, but in seeking the original teaching of Jesus such sayings cannot be relied on. On the other hand, for the Christian it is not only the words of Jesus which are important, but their understanding in the inspired tradition of the Christian community.

2 MARK'S TECHNIQUES IN WRITING

Every writer has tricks of style and ways of writing which are more or less easily recognisable. There are certain techniques which occur so frequently and so pointedly in Mark that they must be considered hallmarks of his own composition. Receiving material from the oral tradition, Mark shaped it in his own way.

The Markan sandwich

Mark often folds one story inside the two halves of another – sometimes for a dramatic purpose, sometimes to stress the theological message, sometimes to mark a contrast. The most obvious instances are these.

1. *Mark 2:1–12* The Cure of a Paralytic, the miracle story, sandwiches the controversy story about forgiveness of sins, in order to stress Jesus' authority.

2. *Mark 3:20–35* The contrasting pieces about Jesus' true kinsfolk sandwich the controversy with the scribes, in order to show the variety of support and opposition to him.

3. *Mark 5:21–43* The Raising of Jairus' Daughter sandwiches the Cure of the Woman with a Haemorrhage, to heighten the dramatic tension of the delay before arriving at Jairus' house.

4. *Mark 6:7–30* The death of John the Baptist is sandwiched between the mission and return of the disciples, to give the illusion of time for their mission. Perhaps it also serves to hint that suffering and death are inevitable concomitants of preaching the message of Jesus.

5. *Mark 11:12–25* The Cursing of the Fig Tree and the Withering of the Fig Tree sandwich the Purging of the Temple, as a symbol of the barrenness of Israel.

6. *Mark 14:53–72* Peter's Denial sandwiches Jesus' stand before the

High Priest in order to highlight the contrast between Jesus' steadfastness and Peter's failure.

The chiasmus

The chiasmus is a figure much used in ancient literature, both Hellenistic
and Hebrew. It is named after the Greek letter 'chi', which has the
form of an X, because of the crossover in the middle. Alternatively, it
may be likened to onion skins, the first member balancing the last, the
second balancing the penultimate, and so on: a-b-c-d-c'-b'-a'- (or any
symmetrical number of members). The stress is usually on the central
member.

Here is one instance:

a 2:1–12: The Cure of a Paralytic, a controversy within a miracle
story
  b 2:13–17: A food controversy, which ends with a proverb on
  mission
    c 2:18–22: The incident of new wineskins, itself a chiasmus:
      a 2:19: A double saying about fasting
        b 2:20: An allusion to the Passion
      a' 2:21: A double saying about new wineskins
  b' 2:23–8: A food controversy, which ends with a proverb on
  authority
a' 3:1–6: The Cure of a Man with a Withered Hand, a controversy
within a miracle story, ending with the threat of the Passion

The purpose of this arrangement, centred on and climaxing in mention
of the Passion, would be to show that already the opposition to Jesus
forebodes its lethal outcome.

The final challenge between Jesus and the Jewish authorities, leading
up to the Passion, may also be read as a chiasmus, centred on the failure
to understand the Resurrection, and bracketed by condemnation of the
Jewish authorities:

a 12:1–9: Judgement on the authorities (parable of the Wicked
Tenants)
  b 12:10–12: Quotation from a psalm (the cornerstone)
    c 12:13–17: Duties to God and to Caesar
      d 12:18–27: Failure to understand the Resurrection
    c' 12:28–34: Duties of love to God and one's neighbour
  b' 12:35–37a: Quotation from a psalm (the son of David)
a' 12:37b–40: A warning against the scribes

Markan threesomes

Another formal pattern in Mark is triple repetition. This is a common feature of folk literature (e.g. Little Red Riding Hood, the Wolf and the Three Little Pigs, the Three Bears, and Dick Whittington and the three peals of bells). Certain characteristics of the grammar and vocabulary used in these constructions are unmistakably Markan. As do folk stories, Mark must have taken these motifs and repeated them in order to emphasise them by the triple repetition.

1. The three great prophecies of the Passion (8:31; 9:31; 10:33), underlining Jesus' foreknowledge and steadfastness.
2. Jesus' three returns to the sleeping disciples in Gethsemane (14:37, 40, 41), stressing the failure of the disciples.
3. The three accusations against Jesus before the High Priest (14:56, 57, 60).
4. Peter's three denials (14:68, 70, 71), stressing his failure.
5. Pilate's three appeals to the crowd in order to have Jesus set free (15:9, 12, 14), emphasising his conviction of Jesus' innocence.
6. The divisions of time at the Crucifixion, the third hour (15:25), the sixth hour (15:33), and the ninth hour (15:34).

Markan style and vocabulary

There are several features of Mark's way of writing which clearly characterise his gospel. Many of these are discernible only in Greek, being matters of vocabulary or construction, and others are often ironed out in translation, since literary translations aim to produce a smoother and more polished effect than Mark offers.

Mark writes the sort of Greek which would have been spoken by the slave population around the Mediterranean. It is quite unsophisticated, in a simple way which makes it interesting to contrast with two other common classes of literature known in the contemporary Hellenistic world (see chapter 9). On the one hand there are the frequent little scientific treatises, by no means ambitious from the literary point of view, on architecture, medicine, warfare, geography and other subjects. On the other hand come the romantic station-bookstall type novels (the hero and heroine meet and fall in love, she is captured and enslaved, after various adventures he wins her back, etc.), current at around that time also. All of these are far more polished than Mark. The other two synoptic evangelists certainly found his style primitive, and constantly improved and corrected it.

Features which do come through in translation include the following.

1. *Parataxis instead of syntaxis* Rather than use subordinate clauses, despite the possibility when occasion – as it often does – offers, Mark gives an endless series of parallel short sentences, joined by 'And' or (twenty-six times) 'Again'. In Chapter 1 alone he uses 'And immediately' nine times. (This is the kind of detail often lost in translation.)

2. *The historic present* Phrases such as 'and he says to them', 'and some people come to him and say to him' (2:18), etc. It can produce a breathless effect, which is not particularly intended. This tense, much used by children and primitive storytellers, is avoided by the other evangelists.

3. *Duality* Mark's thought very frequently proceeds in two steps; sometimes this is repetitious, sometimes the second defines and focuses the first: 'That evening, after sunset' (1:32); 'In the morning, long before dawn' (1:35); 'the skin-disease left him and he was cleansed' (1:42).

4. *Afterthoughts* Mark often offers an explanation of what has gone before, when it would have been more logical – but not necessarily, of course, more effective – to explain beforehand. These explanations can often be bracketed off: 'for they were fishermen' (1:16), 'for there were many of them among his followers' (2:15).

5. *Visualisation* Much of the charm of Mark comes from the visual effect he produces. He has the storyteller's knack of making scenes easy to picture, especially with one imaginable object: Jesus' head on the cushion (4:38); the pitiable antics of the Gerasene demoniac (5:3–5); the little girl walking about (5:42); the gruesome head on the dish (6:28).

These could all be contributory reasons why Mark was chosen personally to tell the story for, to and on behalf of the community. It may be true that he received the stories from the oral tradition 'polished like stones on the seashore', as the form critics said, but he has made them attractive in his own way and given them the stamp of his own narrative style.

3 BIBLIOGRAPHY

On the notion of 'gospel':

Stuhlmacher, P., 'The gospel and the gospels', and Guelich, Robert, 'The gospel genre', in P. Stuhlmacher (ed.), *The Gospel and the Gospels*, Grand Rapids, Eerdmans, 1991.

For a very useful presentation and discussion of the criteria for the authenticity of Jesus' words and actions in the gospel:

Meier, John P., *A Marginal Jew*, New York, Doubleday, 1991, pp. 170–84.

Most of the works on Mark's style require at least a working knowledge of Greek, though some clever work can be done by intelligent use of the references given.

Allen, W. C., *Oxford Studies in the Synoptic Problem*, Oxford, 1911. This has an interesting list of 'Aramaisms in St Mark' (pp. 295–6).

Doudna, J. C., *The Greek of the Gospel of Mark* [Journal of Biblical Literature Monograph Series, XII], Boston, 1961.

Hawkins, Sir John C., *Horae Synopticae*, Oxford, Clarendon, 1909. This is still a fascinating inventory of Markan characteristics with a list of Mark's characteristic words.

Neirynck, F., *Duality in Mark*, Leuven University Press, 1982 (Bulletin of Ephemerides Theologicae Lodanienses 31), revised 1988. This is reasonably intelligible without Greek.

Pryke, E. J., *Redactional Style in the Markan Gospel*, Cambridge, Cambridge University Press, 1978 [Society for New Testament Studies Monograph Series 33]. This is a mine of information.

Turner, C. H., 'Markan usage', articles in *Journal of Theological Studies* **25–7** (1924–1927).

4 PERSONAL STUDY

1. Mark into your work copy of the gospel the features noted in section 2 of this chapter. Henceforward, as you work through this book,

always look up each passage quoted, check that it does prove the
point it claims to prove, and make some note in the text.

2. Find and list some instances of the five features listed on pages 34–8
   – perhaps two of each.

3. In view of Mark's approach to the message of Jesus, what sort of
   person do you imagine him to have been? Write a pen-portrait
   (about one page).

CHAPTER 4

WHY DID MARK WRITE
HIS GOSPEL?

Mark received his material from the oral tradition current in the Christian communities. He collected the stories and sayings, possibly including some pre-existing groups of stories, and shaped them for the benefit of the Christian community in his own way and for his own purposes. But why, and from what angle, did he shape his material in just this way? What did he want to emphasise about Jesus and his Good News? If we can uncover his exact purpose in writing a gospel, many features of the gospel will fall into place.

During this century, since the advent of form criticism, it has been a primary concern of scholars to attempt to reach an understanding of the gospel material by setting the individual pieces back in the situation in which they arose, or the circumstances in which the separate stories are told. The same work can be done on the gospels as wholes. Each will have been written in specific circumstances and against a specific background. We can today understand the various emphases of a piece of writing if we can recover or reconstruct the original thrust of the author, what that author was setting out to prove – a theme which was or is seen to be important at the time of writing.

1 THEORIES

The influential Professor S. G. F. Brandon of Manchester suggested that the real Jesus was in fact a revolutionary leader, one of many revolutionary leaders towards the end of Roman rule in Palestine, attempting to overthrow the Roman domination. Such movements, led by Zealots, eventually (in AD 66) provoked the Roman reaction of besieging and sacking Jerusalem. According to Brandon, it was after this that Jesus' followers, refugees from Jerusalem to Rome, rewrote the history of Jesus to represent him not as a political revolutionary, but as a religious leader.

A more important theory was put forward by Theodore J. Weedon in his 1968 article, 'The heresy that necessitated Mark's gospel'.[1] Weedon noted two important features of Mark, the stress on suffering and persecution, and the stress on the failure of the disciples to understand Jesus' message. Each of these plays an important role in Mark. Weedon saw the gospel as composed to correct a view of Jesus which interpreted him as principally a miracle-worker. There were current at the time stories about various figures ∶ the Hellenistic world who were renowned as miracle-workers, the most prominent of whom was Apollonius of Tyana. The theory is that a certain group of disciples limited their understanding (their 'Heresy') of Jesus to this: they saw the miracles and extraordinary phenomena which occurred in the Christian communities as being the central feature of Christianity. Consequently they regarded the miracles as the feature of Jesus' own life story which was of paramount importance. Certainly Paul, writing to the Corinthians, is hesitant with regard to the extraordinary and to the working of miracles. This does suggest that some Christians placed too much stress on them. According to Weedon, Mark's purpose was to show this group that their conception of Jesus and of Christianity was inadequate: the true view of Jesus was as a suffering Messiah, and true Christianity must involve the followers of Jesus sharing his suffering. In order to teach these lessons by his gospel, Mark lays his emphasis on two points:

1. Even the first disciples were slow to understand, and frequently failed to understand at all. This might suggest that other disciples – namely the leaders of the group who centred all their Christianity on miracles – could also be in the wrong.
2. Suffering was central to Jesus' mission, and he taught that his disciples must share this suffering with him.

---

[1] Most easily available in a collection of essays edited by W. Telford, *The Interpretation of Mark* (Edinburgh, T. & T. Clark, 1995).

2 THE UNRESPONSIVE DISCIPLES

The shape of Mark's gospel, like so many of his individual expressions, is bipartite. For the first half of the gospel, up to the scene at Caesarea Philippi (8:27–30), the disciples are painfully and slowly coming to a realisation that Jesus is the Messiah. From that time onwards they are discovering, equally slowly, that his messiahship involves suffering and persecution. In each half, however, the slowness of the disciples to grasp the message of their Master is a striking feature. There is a sharp division in this between the reader of the gospel and the actors in the drama: the reader knows from the very beginning that Jesus is the Christ (1:1). Jesus' special quality is declared also by the voice from heaven at the Baptism and at the Transfiguration. The unclean spirits cast out by Jesus declare it also. Yet at the same time the reader can see the disciples again and again failing to understand the significance of events and of Jesus himself. This dramatic irony, the movement of the gospel on two levels, is a feature of Mark's presentation.

The failure of the disciples in different ways gets worse and worse throughout the gospel. At the end there is a reconciliation, consisting in the meeting in Galilee implied by the angel's message. But, even so, it is not clear that they are totally trusted; there is no such final commission to go and teach all nations as there is in the last few verses of Matthew.

Theodore T. Weedon charts the three stages of the progressive deterioration of the disciples. In the first stage of the gospel the portrait is reasonably positive: the first four are called and respond immediately and without question (1:16–20). They are called to be with Jesus and to go out and proclaim, with power to expel evil spirits (3:13–15). They are the privileged recipients of the mystery of the kingship (4:11). They are sent out on their mission, which they fulfil (6:12–13) and seem to receive Jesus' congratulations on returning (6:30–1).

Yet even at this early stage all is not well. In direct contrast to his previous distinction between insiders who understand the mystery and outsiders who don't (3:31–5), after the first parable Jesus shows disappointment that the disciples do not understand the parable of the Sower and will therefore be incapable of understanding 'all' (which may mean 'any') of the parables (4:13).

They fail to rely calmly on Jesus in the storm on the lake, though the fact that they turn to him at all shows a certain amount of trust; nevertheless there is a sharp exchange, the disciples treating Jesus to sarcasm ('Master, do you not care?') and Jesus replying with the accusation of cowardice (4:38–40). In the story of the Woman with a

Haemorrhage they are again sarcastic: 'You see how the crowd is pressing round you; how can you ask, "Who touched me?" ' (5:31). At the first Multiplication of Loaves they fail to appreciate Jesus' power to solve the difficulty, and douse him with sarcasm (6:37): 'Are we supposed [deliberative subjunctive] to go off and buy . . .?' Their failure to understand about the Multiplication of Loaves is pointed by Mark, for without the finale of 6:52 the story of the Walking on the Water could merely show reverential awe of the right kind: 'They were utterly and completely dumbfounded, because they had not seen what the miracle of the loaves meant; their minds were closed.'

After the dispute over the tradition of the elders the disciples' lack of comprehension is again underlined by the Markan dual phrase, 'Even you – don't you understand? Can't you see that . . .?' (7:18). Jesus could have given further instruction without any such remark, simply moving 'into the house', and his words are woundingly framed.

Finally, in the discussion after the second Bread Miracle, they totally fail to understand the situation, again eliciting a Markan double question (one of the frequent features of Mark's gospel, and surely an indication that he is writing this passage himself): 'Do you still not understand, still not realise?' (8:17). Even Peter's confession at Caesarea Philippi shows deep misunderstanding:[2] he recognises that Jesus is the Christ, but misunderstands Jesus' real purpose to the extent of rebuking him and tempting him in the way Satan does (8:29–33).

In the second half of the gospel they are equally slow to understand the message of suffering (see below). They also fail in the task they were given as exorcists (9:18), and starkly disobey the instruction (9:37) to welcome children (10:13–16), thereby earning Jesus' annoyance (cf. the disciples' indignation in 14:4–6).

This strikingly critical attitude of Mark to the disciples is brought into even sharper focus through its omission by Matthew and Luke. The evangelists who use Mark as their basis and adjust his text for their own purposes, to express their own insights of Jesus, shy away from such strong criticism. After the Walking on the Water, instead of Mark's note of complete puzzlement (6:52), Matthew shows the disciples worshipping Jesus as Son of God (14:33). Instead of the prolonged criticism by Jesus at Mark 8:17–18, Matthew has the much milder rebuke of 16:9. Instead of the ambitious and arrogant request of the sons of Zebedee, Matthew puts the request in their mother's mouth. On every occasion the sarcasm of the disciples and any sharpness in

---

[2] Jerry Camery-Hoggatt, in his illuminating study, *Irony in Mark's Gospel* (Cambridge, CUP, 1992), calls it 'the deepest irony in the book' (p. 155).

Jesus' rebuke to them are toned down. It looks as though the later evangelist had more respect for the first leaders of the Christian community than did Mark, and was unwilling to allow them to be seen in such an unfavourable light.

3 THE IMPORTANCE OF SUFFERING AND PERSECUTION

The first part of the gospel

Another strong emphasis in the gospel of Mark is on suffering. It is for this reason that Martin Kähler called the gospel a Passion Narrative with an extended introduction. Already in the first half of the gospel there are indications that Jesus is to suffer. The first group of controversies with the Pharisees, so carefully constructed on a chiasmus (2:1—3:6, see page 35), ends with the threat of the Passion: 'The Pharisees went out and began at once to plot with the Herodians against him, discussing how to destroy him.' This threat hangs over the whole of the gospel story, so that the reader cannot forget the final outcome. The story of the death of the Baptist, also carefully placed by Mark, is a further hint of what is to come. Right at the beginning Jesus is placed in parallel with the Baptist: both preach repentance (the Baptist in 1:4, Jesus in 1:15), the Baptist as part of his heralding of the kingdom, Jesus as part of his proclamation of the kingdom close at hand. The parallel is further stressed in the preface to the story of the beheading of the Baptist, when King Herod sees in Jesus a reappearance of the Baptist (6:16), and by the sandwiching of the death of the Baptist in the middle of the first mission to preach the gospel (page 34).

Towards the Passion

At the turning point constituted by the incident at Caesarea Philippi, once Peter has acknowledged Jesus as 'the Christ', immediately Jesus begins to announce the Passion. The three great formal prophecies of the Passion (8:31; 9:31; 10:33) punctuate the run-up to the final climax. Each of these is followed by a failure of the disciples to understand this message, and a reiteration by Jesus that his disciples must follow his path.

1. First Peter attempts to divert Jesus from his purpose, and is vigorously rebuked, 'Get behind me, Satan!' (8:33). Jesus then makes clear that his disciples must renounce themselves and take up their cross (8:34–7).
2. After the second prophecy immediately the disciples show their imperviousness to this message by arguing about precedence in the kingdom (9:34). To this Jesus ripostes, 'If anyone wants to be first, he must make himself last of all and servant of all' (9:35).
3. After the third comes the similar scene of the sons of Zebedee asking for the chief places in the kingdom (10:35–7). Jesus replies that he can offer them only his own cup of suffering (10:39).

Thus each time Mark emphasises the place of suffering in the Christian community by showing the reluctance of the disciples to accept the message, and reiterates that they too must share it with Jesus.

The eschatological discourse

Immediately before the story of the Passion itself begins, Mark has placed his great Chapter 13, the longest single presentation of Jesus' teaching in the gospel, concerning the future of his community.

The apocalypse

This presentation is in the well-known form of an apocalypse. The standard circumstance of an apocalypse, from the Book of Daniel onwards, is a situation of persecution. Daniel itself was written during the great persecution of Antiochus Epiphanes, to reassure its readers that persecution was sure to happen, and that in the end God would rescue his elect. The Apocalypse or Revelation of John must be situated in the Roman persecutions towards the end of the first century, again promising final triumph and the bliss of the new and eschatological Jerusalem (Rv 21—22). Contemporary with Jesus were many such apocalyptic writings, reacting to the harsh and detested Roman rule in Palestine, and promising that persecution was only temporary, and would issue in the deliverance and triumph of the people of God.

Similarly Mark 13 shows Jesus prophesying that his followers will be persecuted, but that finally the Son of man will come in the clouds (the symbol of God's power and presence) and 'will send the angels to gather his elect from the four winds, from the ends of the world to the ends of the sky' (13:27).

The account of the Passion

The Agony in the Garden

When we come to the Passion story itself, the very first introductory scene, the Agony in the Garden, again contrasts Jesus and his disciples. This again is a scene constructed by Mark. That much is clear not only from the structure of triple repetition itself, but from the Markan style and vocabulary evident particularly at crucial points of it. The striking point is that it is not Jesus' prayer that is most prominent, but his return to the sleeping disciples. What Mark wishes to stress is not so much Jesus' own willingness to offer himself to the Father's will, despite his overwhelming horror at and shrinking from death, but the failure of the disciples to share with him.

Mark has the same prayer as John 12:27, but in a slightly different form, 'Father! . . . Take this cup away from me. But let it be as you, not I, would have it' (Mk 14:36). The fact that the emphasis is on the failure of the disciples rather than on Jesus' prayer is evident from the details of Mark's description. Mark gives no content to the second prayer, saying only, 'Again he went away and prayed, saying the same words.' For the third instance even this is lacking. But what does occur each of the three times is Jesus' return to find the disciples sleeping (vv. 37, 40, 41). At the end of the scene the contrast is made even more poignant, as Jesus and his disciples part in opposite directions, the disciples running away and deserting Jesus, and Jesus himself being led off to the High Priest.

The hearing before the High Priest

In the following scene Mark has stressed the same lesson. He sandwiches Jesus' stance before the High Priest between the two halves of Peter's triple denial (two characteristics of Mark's composition, the sandwich and the threesome). Before the hearing begins, Peter is already in position (v. 54). After the series of three accusations against Jesus come the three denials themselves, increasing in vehemence (vv. 68, 70, 71). Again the triple shape and the lack of material suggest that Mark himself must have built the scene into its present form. There is no need to

question the lively, circumstantial and detailed story of the servant-girl
and the gibe of Peter betraying himself as a Galilean by his speech.
These are just the sort of details at which Mark excels, his genius for
storytelling coming to the fore: it is as vivid as the best of the Markan
confrontations, like the disciples approaching Jesus as he lies asleep in
the boat, 'his head on the cushion' (4:38), or the tragic antics of the
Gerasene demoniac (5:3–5), or the revived little girl tripping around
(5:42), or the gruesome head on a dish (6:28). Here, though, as in the
Agony in the Garden, Mark seems to lack further details: besides
the scene with the girl he offers practically only 'he denied it', 'again
he denied it'. It seems as though here Mark has divided his detailed
information between the first and the third denials. Attention is almost
more on Peter than on Jesus himself: the final climax of the whole
scene is nothing to do with Jesus, but the collapse of Peter: 'And he
burst into tears.'

This is the last mention of any of Jesus' chosen disciples until the
promise of reconciliation in the very final scene of the gospel: 'you
must go and tell his disciples and Peter, "He is going ahead of you to
Galilee; that is where you will see him . . ." ' (16:7).

4 THE PORTRAIT OF THE DISCIPLES

Ernest Best[3] rejects the explanation that Mark is writing to correct a
group of heretical Christians on the grounds that if this were the case
there should be another group visible with whom the erring disciples
would be contrasted. For example, if they stood for the ministers of the
community contrasted with people as a whole, there would be another
group represented who did understand. As it is, the disciples (or the
Twelve) seem to stand for Christian disciples as a whole. It is hard to
believe that Mark sees the whole community as captivated by this
preoccupation with miracles to the exclusion of all else. There is no
reason to suppose that Mark was necessarily writing to correct any
wrong impression.

So Best prefers a pedagogical explanation: the gospel is concerned
with the difficulty of assimilating Jesus' message. Mark wishes to stress
the wonder of the Jesus-event by underlining how hard it was to
understand. Matthew and Luke, in contrast, can remove the tough
criticism of the disciples because they do not lay such stress on amaze-

---

[3] Ernest Best, *Disciples and Discipleship* (Edinburgh, T. & T. Clark, 1986), and his article
'The role of the disciples in Mark', *New Testament Studies* 23, (1976/77), p. 377–401.

ment at the Jesus-event. To this Best adds a pastoral aspect: the lesson of suffering is not easy to learn; not only the leaders but the whole community must have found it difficult to assimilate. This is the reason for the generalisation of criticisms, aimed at instructing the community as a whole. Thus Mark adds to the incomprehension of Peter at the Transfiguration ('He did not know what to say', 9:6) a wider phrase which could be aimed at the whole community, 'they were so frightened.' When Peter swears loyalty (14:31), Mark adds, 'And they all said the same.' When Simon is reproached (14:37), 'Had you not the strength to stay awake one hour?', the admonition follows in the plural (and is therefore directed not at a single person but at many), 'Stay awake and pray . . .'.

One further aspect of Mark's teaching method may be mentioned. The reader is meant to identify with the disciples, which is why the initial presentation is so positive. Only after so identifying is the reader led to become self-critical and aware of personal failures, as seen also in the disciples. Thus Jesus' special choice of the disciples to be close to him is stressed, and there is a final reconciliation after the Resurrection in the implied invitation to join the Risen Christ in Galilee (16:7, prepared also by 14:27–8). In this way the reader is drawn into the experience of the disciples, both their closeness to Jesus and their difficulty in assimilating his message.

5 CHANCE COMERS ATTRACTED TO JESUS

Another striking fact, to which none of the explanations of Mark's purpose discussed draws attention, is the contrast between the specially selected and carefully privileged group of disciples and others who encounter Jesus. During the early, positive, presentation of the disciples their openness to the mystery is contrasted with the inability of outsiders to hear and understand. Similarly 'those around Jesus' are contrasted with his own blood relations (3:31–5). But later there does seem to be a deliberate contrast in the opposite direction, as in 6:53–6. Time and again individuals show their faith and are commended by Jesus. The woman with a haemorrhage has the faith to know that the touch of Jesus will cure her; in this she contrasts with the sarcastic disciples, who seem unaware that the touch can have any significance (5:31). The Syro-Phoenician woman wins commendation and a cure by her wit, founded on faith and understanding of Jesus (7:24–30). The father of the epileptic demoniac brings his son to the disciples, yet they cannot cure the boy (9:18). Are the disciples the object envisaged by Jesus' exasperated comment (a Markan double question), 'Faithless generation, how much longer must I be among you? How much longer must I put up with you?' People bring little children to Jesus, the disciples scold them, and Jesus indignantly says (again with Markan duality), 'Let the little children come to me; do not stop them' (10:14). The sons of Zebedee show their ambition, and immediately afterwards Bartimaeus, as they leave Jericho, expresses his faith (10:35–8, 46–52). The woman at Bethany lavishes ointment on him, but those with him are indignant at the waste (14:4). One might add Simon of Cyrene, enlisted willingly or unwillingly to carry the cross when the disciples have deserted him (15:21), and Joseph of Arimathaea who fulfils the relatives' duty of burying him (15:46).

In some of these cases the disciples may be regarded as a pedagogical foil or dramatic dummies to bring out the message more clearly, as though Mark feels that the reader must already be so convinced of the disciples' faithfulness that they can now take some flak. But the constant repetition of this procedure does make it at best clumsy and tactless. The editorial stressing of the contrast must have a purpose. The solution is twofold. The first clue must lie in Mark 13:11, 'do not worry beforehand about what to say; no, say whatever is given to you when the time comes, because it is not you who will be speaking; it is the Holy Spirit.' In order to show the importance of the role of the Holy Spirit, the incapacity of the disciples – and particularly of Peter, their leader – when left on their own is exploited to the full.

The second clue is that Mark wishes to show that an immediate and passing response to Jesus is easy enough. The initial response to the Word, as in the parable of the Sower, is to welcome it with joy (4:16); such a situation is reflected in the welcome given to Jesus by the chance comers. It is only later, when persecution and distraction come, that the task becomes more difficult. Matthew and Luke use a whole string of parables: Mark, who is in general much more sparing in giving Jesus' teaching, has only two major parables to illustrate a point. One may therefore presume that any point illustrated by a parable is an important one. The Sower therefore illustrates the variety of responses and the difficulties of the process of growth after the initial welcome. It is a microcosm of the difficulty of the disciples, seen also in the rest of the gospel. This is made clear in the explanation given in 4:13–20.

6 MARK'S COMMUNITY

It would be interesting to be able to deduce from the gospel more information about the community for which Mark wrote, as Raymond E. Brown has done in *The Community of the Beloved Disciple* (London, Geoffrey Chapman, 1979), using shrewd detective-work on the Johannine writings. We can see that it was a community for which persecution and defection were problems. That was why they needed encouragement to see that persecution was inevitable for Christians, and that it was hard to take, or even to understand. It was perhaps because some of their members had defected under persecution that Mark stresses so strongly that even the disciples and their leader had failed under persecution, despite their protestations of loyalty.

Is it possible to go further and argue from the stress on service that Mark's community were prone to self-aggrandisement, and needed special stress on the lesson of humility and of Christian dignity through service? There is a certain danger in mirror-reading – that is, in assuming that every stress by Mark corresponds to a lacuna in his community.

Some would claim from the presence of Latin loan-words in Mark (*kenturion*, and the like), that the gospel was written in Italy or even in Rome. But Roman culture and language were so widespread around the Mediterranean that such deductions would be unjustified. It is not only Americans who speak of Coca-Cola, nor are all culs-de-sac in France.

7 BIBLIOGRAPHY

Telford, W., (ed.), *The Interpretation of Mark*, Edinburgh, T. & T. Clark, 1995. See especially the essays by Theodore J. Weedon, 'The heresy that necessitated Mark's gospel', and by Ernest Best, 'The role of the disciples in Mark'.

8 PERSONAL STUDY

Write an essay (two or three pages) in response to the question, 'Why is Mark so hard on the disciples?' Mention and discuss a couple of theories on the matter, as well as your own view. Give references to Mark for each point made.

CHAPTER 5

THE KINGSHIP OF GOD IN MARK

'. . . the kingdom of God is close at hand. Repent, and believe the gospel' (Mk 1:15). With this proclamation Jesus' preaching begins. But the content of this proclamation and the nature of the kingdom envisaged by Jesus have remained hotly disputed.

1 THE PROBLEM – MODERN VIEWS

Albert Schweitzer

At the beginning of this century Albert Schweitzer, the great Swiss theologian and organist, and later the founder of a leper colony and winner of the Nobel Peace Prize, propounded a theory which has influenced theology and which has been continually discussed ever since. He maintained that Jesus urgently expected a cosmic cataclysm, the break-up of the present structure of the world. He sent out his disciples with no time to lose, expecting that their preaching would usher in the final stage of the world. When they returned without this having been fulfilled, he revised his view and took the sufferings of the final cataclysm on himself. He wrongly expected his Passion and death to be the last act in the drama of renewal of the cosmos. He thought that with his death the world as people knew it would come to an end, and a new world order, expected by the Jews, would begin.

Schweitzer's view was massively influential, and was accepted in essence by the other great influence on twentieth century gospel scholarship, the form-critical school. Despite its far-reaching corollaries for the view of Jesus himself, the inevitable consequence was accepted: that

Jesus' central vision, and his state of mind as he went to his death, were wrong. Yet even at the time voices were raised to question its basis: had Schweitzer really interpreted correctly the current Jewish ideas of the final cataclysm and the world to come? R. H. Charles, whose knowledge of first century Jewish writings was unrivalled, wrote, 'Schweitzer's eschatological studies show no knowledge of the original documents and hardly any of first-hand work on the documents'.

Norman Perrin

Half a century after Schweitzer the British-American scholar Norman Perrin held that 'the kingdom of God' in the preaching of Jesus was a mythical formulation which needed to be interpreted as a sort of symbol or cypher for God's power at work in the world. According to Perrin, the kingdom of God is a personal challenge to every Christian. It is not 'a single identifiable reality which every man experiences at the same time, but something which every man experiences in his own time'.[1]

E. P. Sanders

More recently E. P. Sanders, in a series of works, has seen Jesus' preaching in the context of the renewal of Judaism expected in the late biblical and post-biblical writings, a this-worldly rather than an other-worldly phenomenon. Jesus intended to establish a structure and a society, a politico-religious entity. At least some views of the renewal of Judaism, which was to be achieved by the visitation of God, envisaged it as occurring within the present spatio-temporal constitution of the world, rather than as bringing this structure to an end. If Jesus made arrangements for the continuance of the society he had founded, then he did not expect the world as we know it to come to an end at his death.

2 THE OLD TESTAMENT AND THE INTER-TESTAMENTAL PERIOD

The term: kingdom or kingship?

The term 'kingdom', which is commonly used, can suggest a territorial entity like the kingdom of Spain. This is reinforced by Matthew's

---

[1] Norman Perrin, *Journal of Biblical Literature* **93** (1974), p. 13.

expression 'the kingdom of heaven', which suggests that the kingdom of God is located in heaven. In fact Matthew uses this expression only out of Jewish reverence: Matthew was following the Jewish practice, already current in the first century, of avoiding the use of the word 'God' out of reverence. 'Heaven', thought of as the seat of God, was commonly used instead of the word 'God'.

The Hebrew word *malkuth*, which is at the base of the expression, is an abstract noun denoting not a territorial entity but the fact of God being king, or the royal power of God. If one word is sought, perhaps the 'sovereignty' or 'kingship' of God is best. Others have translated it simply 'the revolution'. Whatever the translation, it is important to realise that the stress is not so much on the word – 'kingdom', 'kingship', or 'revolution' – as on the fact that it is bringing God into due prominence. The stress is on God. So R. T. France entitled his book on the concept in Mark '*Divine Government*'.

The kingship of God in the Old Testament

That God is king of Israel is basic to the thinking of the Old Testament, and comes to expression at least from the beginning of the monarchical period *c.* 1000 BC. Gideon refused to be king when his victorious campaigns against Israel's enemies led him to be offered this post (Jg 8:22–3). Eventually some sort of permanent leadership was forced upon Israel, at the end of the period of the charismatic and temporary Judges, to provide permanent opposition to the incursions of the Philistines.

Saul was anointed king by Samuel in about 1020 BC, but only under protest from the prophet, who regarded this assimilation to the structure of other nations as casting doubt on the effectiveness of Yahweh's protection of his people. For Samuel, Yahweh alone is king. When the Israelites demand that Samuel should anoint a king for them, Yahweh says to him, 'it is not you they have rejected but me, not wishing me to reign over them any more' (1 S 8:8). Samuel follows this up with a recital of the evils and abuses to which a human king will subject the nation (1 S 8:10–22).

When David became king – by fair means or foul – he ensured that he was regarded very firmly as the Lord's anointed, punishing the mercy-killer of Saul as the murderer of the Lord's anointed (2 S 1:16), and making his personal capital the holy city of Yahweh by installing the Ark there (2 S 6). He ruled there as the vice-regent of Yahweh. A very ancient psalm sings of the coronation of a king as his adoption to be son of God (Ps 110:3). A whole series of psalms sung in the Temple of Jerusalem celebrate the sovereignty of Yahweh:

> Great is Yahweh and most worthy of praise
>   in the city of our God . . .
> Mount Zion in the heart of the north,
>   the settlement of the great king . . .   (Ps 48:1–2)

> Yahweh is king, robed in majesty,
> robed is Yahweh and girded with power.   (Ps 93:1)

> Yahweh is king, the peoples tremble;
> he is enthroned on the winged creatures, the earth shivers;
> Yahweh is great in Zion.   (Ps 99:1)

(See also Psalms 96, 97, 145 and 146.)

As time went on, and particularly from the era of the Babylonian Exile, Israel became aware that the kingship of Yahweh embraced not just themselves but the whole world. Until the Exile Yahweh had been conceived primarily as the God of Israel, Israel's special protector. The question of the relationship of Yahweh to other nations had not become an important issue. At the Sack of Jerusalem in 597 BC one of the shattering blows to Israel was that Yahweh was unable (or unwilling) to protect his people as a king should. It was the king's business to keep his nation secure, and Yahweh had failed in this. As Ezekiel puts it (36:20–2), his name had been 'profaned . . . among the nations' – that is, his reputation as king and protector of Israel had been tarnished.

But the Exile was a time for new insights, and in exile, confronted with the plethora of gods at Babylon, Israel was forced to question the relationship of Yahweh to other gods, to the protectors of other nations, and to the deities which the Babylonians claimed ruled various aspects of the world and of daily life. Israel reacted by asserting strongly for the first time that Yahweh is the creator and ruler of the whole universe, and this assertion was expressed in terms of Yahweh's kingship. This is especially a theme of the prophet of the Exile, Deutero-Isaiah:

> Thus says Yahweh, Israel's king,
> Yahweh Sabaoth, his redeemer:
> I am the first, I am the last;
> there is no God except me.   (Is 44:6; cf. Is 43:15; 52:7)

Finally, at the end of the Old Testament period, comes the expectation of a final, victorious coming of God as king. This is a combination of the ancient theme of the Day of the Lord – a day of God's visitation of the earth to correct wrongs and rescue his chosen ones – with the theme of kingship. By now it has taken on universal dimensions, for God deserves worship from all the nations of the world, and failure to worship him will bring them punishment:

> When that Day comes, living waters will issue from Jerusalem, half towards the eastern sea, half towards the western sea; they will flow summer and winter. Then Yahweh will become king of the whole world. . . .
>
> After this, all the survivors of all the nations which have attacked Jerusalem will come up year after year to worship the King, Yahweh Sabaoth, and to keep the feast of Shelters. Should one of the races of the world fail to come up to Jerusalem to worship the King, Yahweh Sabaoth, there will be no rain for that one.
>
> (Zc 14:8–9, 16–17)

The kingship of God in first-century Palestine

In the century before Christ there was a lively expectation of some decisive event by which God would break into world history. This is to be found in many different circles of Judaism.

The *Psalms of Solomon* were written in the latter part of the first century before Christ. Psalm 17 concentrates on a Davidic king, a representative of the Lord, who will purge Jerusalem of the foreigners who oppress it. He will gather together and lead a holy people, who will hope in the Lord and form a centre for all the peoples of the earth:

> Raise up unto them their king, the son of David, . . . that he may shatter unrighteous rulers and purge Jerusalem from nations that trample her down. . . . And he shall gather together a holy people whom he shall lead in righteousness. . . . He shall judge nations in the wisdom of his righteousness, and he shall have the heathen nations to serve him under his yoke. . . . The Lord himself is his king, the hope of him that is mighty through his hope in God.

The Assumption of Moses, a similar contemporary work, contains the same combination of themes, associating the kingdom with an end to evil and the punishment of foreigners:

> And then his kingdom shall appear throughout his creation,
> and Satan shall be no more,
> and sorrow shall depart with him . . .
> and he will appear to punish the gentiles　　　(*Ass. Mos.* 10)

In the Scrolls of Qumran one of the most important is the War Scroll, which describes a war between the sons of Light and the sons of Darkness, to take place at the end of time, for the triumph of the faithful and the destruction of the wicked. It is a constant refrain that this war is to the kingly glory of God:

> You are a terrible God in your kingly glory . . .
> For Adonai is holy
> and the king of glory is with us, accompanied by the saints.
> The powers of the hosts of angels are among our men,
> and the valiant in battle is our congregation.   (1 QM 12:7–8)

These are chance quotations from very different milieux. The first is from Pharisaic circles at the centre of Jewish orthodoxy; the last from the sectaries of Qumran, who had fled from precisely such attitudes. They all share these same themes. But they clearly used the language of images, and the question is how this language is to be understood.

There was alive in Jesus' time a lively expectation that a decisive liberation was about to take place. The sectaries who formed a community at Qumran, in revolt against official Jerusalem Judaism, withdrew into the desert area near the Dead Sea in order to await the Messiah, and hopefully laid a place for the Messiah at their daily ritual meal. The expectation was fomented by, and in turn boiled over into, the series of messianic revolts against the Roman rule. From the Jewish historian Josephus we know that at least petty revolts were frequent. One of these was led by Judas the Galilean at about the turn of the eras, another by the messianic claimant known only as 'the Egyptian'. These both promised messianic miracles, such as leading their army dry-shod across the River Jordan. They were, however, swiftly crushed by the Roman military power. Later, after the time of Jesus, the full-scale revolt of AD 66 led to the siege and sacking of Jerusalem by the Romans. Another major abortive messianic revolt broke out in AD 132, led by Simon ben Kosiba (or Bar-Kochba). He was recognised as messiah even by the great Rabbi Aqiba.

3 THE KINGSHIP OF GOD IN MARK

This section is intended to investigate the meaning of the concept 'kingship of God' in Mark's gospel, rather than in Jesus' own thought. Written as it was some decades after Jesus' own preaching, and in different circumstances, Mark's gospel does not necessarily reflect exactly the same emphases as Jesus' original message. The evangelists were theologians, mediating the message of Jesus to Christians in their own time. Rather than simply recording what Jesus had said and done, they interpreted the message of Jesus to their contemporaries. It is a different question to ask how Jesus himself understood the kingship of God, though there must be continuity between the two concepts.

It is striking that the expression 'the kingship of God' occurs much more seldom in Mark than one would expect. In Matthew it is a concept which appears everywhere, occurring some fifty-two times. In Mark, however, it comes no more than fifteen times. It is important, therefore, to avoid confusing the way the term is used in Mark with the more diffuse usage of Matthew. Quite possibly the concept of the kingdom current in Matthew, perhaps reflecting the tensions and interests of the Christian community around him, may be quite different from that found in Mark.

The importance to Mark of the concept of the kingship is clear from the beginning. After the introductory verses the first proclamation of Jesus, which sets the tone for the whole, is that the kingship of God 'is close at hand'. Acceptance of this seems to imply repentance and belief in the gospel (1:15), which is mentioned just before and just after the kingship. The gospel and the kingship are, then, inextricably linked. What this implies is not yet clear.

Two of the questions often posed about the concept are whether the kingship is conceived as present or future (or both), and whether the kingship is something voluntarily accepted or something which bursts upon the world (or both). For the New Testament in general Norman Perrin has collected texts which argue about the timing of the kingship in both directions: in one sense it is already present, in another it is still to come; is the same true for Mark alone? Similarly we must ask whether Mark views the kingship as a spontaneous acceptance of God's will or as a new state of things superimposed by God.

Conditions of entry

One aspect of the concept of the kingship of God is surely a moral one. So much is clear from the initial announcement of the kingship of God. It involves repentance, a change of life (1:15). Furthermore, the kingdom is something which demands certain qualities and to which other qualities tend to be a bar. If one's eye leads one astray morally, it is better to do without the eye and enter the kingdom one-eyed (9:47). Those who wish to enter must be like children (10:15). Riches make entry difficult (10:23–5). The lawyer who recognises the importance of the two commandments of love is 'not far from the kingdom of God'

(12:34). There is no hint here of any long delay, or of any need for an explosive event from God to make entry possible. Incidentally, all these sayings smack of the clarity and the black-and-white quality, the absolute demands, or indeed even what seems to us the exaggeration, of Jesus' own teaching.

Overwhelmingly Paul also uses the term 'kingdom' with moral connotations. You must live a life worthy of the kingdom (1 Th 2:12). The kingdom does not consist in food and drink (Rm 14:17), will not be the inheritance of the people who do evil (1 Co 6:9). In Paul, therefore, just as in Mark, the meaning of 'kingdom' may in one way be understood as a moral response to the message of the gospel.

The miracles

Another aspect of the kingship of God brought by Jesus is, however, the breaking-in of God's presence and action in the world by the triumph over evil, the purification of Israel, and the removal of sorrow and distress, and especially of sin.

One way in which this comes to view in Jesus' ministry is in his conflict with and triumph over evil spirits. This would naturally be seen as a sign of the triumph over evil associated with the arrival of the kingship of God.

Possession by evil spirits

In the popular imagination of the unscientific age, illness was frequently attributed to possession by evil spirits. This is easily understandable at a time when the physical or psychological causes of illness were hardly considered scientifically. Especially in the case of mental illness, it is still only one step from saying that someone is 'not himself/herself' to saying that 'he or she seems to be in the grip of an evil or deranged spirit'.

Unclean spirits

Jesus' triumph over evil spirits is a recurrent theme of the gospel. It is important not only because it shows Jesus' power in these individual cases, but also because it must surely be seen as evidence of Jesus' power over the evil which ruled the world. The expulsion of an unclean spirit is the first wonder worked by Jesus (Mk 1:21–8). The way the expulsion is sandwiched between passages on teaching suggest that Mark himself placed the incident in this significant position. In the summary passages about Jesus' activity, healings and the expulsion of evil spirits feature together (1:32–4; 6:13). The expulsion of the evil spirit from the Gerasene demoniac again is a highly Markan story (5:1–20). Most significant is the passage where the scribes attempt to explain away his expulsions, thereby implicitly granting that he does in fact perform them (3:22–30, again sandwiched, in this case between the two passages on the kinsfolk of Jesus). Here, in his rebuttal, Jesus alludes to the kingdom: 'If a kingdom is divided against itself, that kingdom cannot last.'

Cures

Other illnesses, too, are viewed in the Markan stories as cases of possession. In 1:40–5 Jesus cures a man with a virulent skin-disease.

Skin-diseases

The leprosy of the gospels is not what is today called leprosy (*Mycobacterium leprae*). In the Bible the term covers many afflictions and skin complaints. The legislation about 'leprosy' given in Leviticus 13—14 shows that the term includes at least any contagious or virulent skin-disease.

The narrative suggests that this too is regarded as possession by an evil spirit, for 1:43 should be translated literally, 'And being angry with him/it, Jesus immediately threw him out.' It makes no sense that Jesus should have been angry with the sufferer, or thrown him out, especially after, in 1:41, he has been 'feeling sorry for him'. It makes much better sense if the anger and expulsion are directed at the disease or an evil spirit who is considered responsible for it.

Other wonderful cures by Jesus, bringing an end to the evil of sickness and disease, would also have been regarded as signs of the coming of God's kingship. The healings were:

- of Simon's mother-in-law (1:29–31);
- of the paralytic of Capernaum (2:1–12);
- of the man with a withered hand (3:1–6);
- of the woman with a haemorrhage and of Jairus' daughter (5:21–43);
- of the Syro-Phoenician woman's daughter (7:24–30);
- of the deaf man (7:31–7);
- of the blind man at Bethsaida (8:22–6);
- of the epileptic demoniac (9:14–29);
- of Bartimaeus at Jericho (10:46–52).

The eschatological context

Not all miraculous cures need necessarily be regarded as signs of the coming of God's kingship. Numerous miraculous cures are recorded at the healing shrine of Aesculapius in Greece, in the Greek magical papyri, and in the story of Apollonius of Tyana.[2] About the same time other cures by those attractive figures the charismatic Galilean rabbis are attested in Jewish literature, and carry no such significance. But in the case of Jesus the whole context is different, and points only to this.

When the Baptist appeared, he already proclaimed the approach of the final times. He put himself forward as the final messenger of God by bearing and wearing the signs of Elijah, the hair cloak on the leather loincloth (Mk 1:6) as Elijah had done (2 K 1:8). Elijah was prophesied to precede the final coming: 'Look, I shall send you the prophet Elijah before the great and awesome Day of Yahweh comes' (Ml 3:23). So Jesus' miracles must be seen quite specifically in the context of his proclamation of the kingship of God.

The final coming

This same interpretation is given, only more explicitly, by the passage in Matthew and Luke where the messengers come from the imprisoned John the Baptist to ask whether Jesus is 'the one who is to come': he replies by citing the evidence of his miracles of healing in terms of the prophecy of Isaiah (Mt 11:2–6). The miracles are therefore the fulfilment of these promises in the last times.

---

[2] See David R. Cartlidge and David L. Dungan, *Documents for the Study of the Gospels* (Philadelphia, Fortress Press, 1980), pp. 151–9.

Three decisive sayings of Jesus

There are three decisive sayings of Jesus in Mark which suggest that the realisation of the kingship of God is not to be long delayed.

Before the Transfiguration
Before the Transfiguration Jesus declares (Mk 9:1):

> 'there are some standing here who will not taste death before they see the kingdom of God come with power.'

This is 'one of the most discussed verses in the whole of Mark's gospel'.[3] Firstly a distinction must be made between the original meaning in Jesus' mouth and the meaning which the verse takes in Mark's gospel. In Mark's gospel the striking position surely indicates that Mark is pointing it towards the Transfiguration itself, and regards the Transfiguration as at least partly fulfilling it. In Jesus' mouth, however, there is a difficulty. In what sense can it be said to have been fulfilled? If it was not fulfilled, can Jesus have been wrong in a matter so integral to his message? At Mark 13:32 he says that he does not know the day nor the hour of it; but it is one thing to admit lack of knowledge, and another to claim knowledge which is incorrect. Such questions must wait until a later chapter. At any rate Mark, in giving the saying such a prominent position, must have seen in it some meaning justified by the position.

At the Last Supper
At the Last Supper Jesus says (Mk 14:25),

> 'I shall never drink wine any more until the day I drink the new wine in the kingdom of God.'

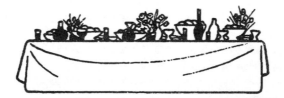

This saying is not part of the original tradition of the institution of the eucharist. The saying must be an independent saying garnered by Mark and deliberately placed here. Luke, who has an independent tradition of the institution, closer to Paul's version than to Mark's, places it before

---

[3] Morna Hooker, *The Gospel of Mark* p. 211.

rather than after the narrative of the institution. It may be, therefore, that Mark placed it here with the intention that the reader should see the fulfilment of this saying in the immediately following Passion and Resurrection account. In this case Mark is suggesting that the fulfilment of the kingship of God in some sense occurs in the Resurrection, just as it occurred in some sense in the Transfiguration.

Before the High Priest

Before the High Priest Jesus replies (Mk 14:62):

> 'you will see the Son of man seated at the right hand of the Power and coming with the clouds of heaven.'

Here it is the 'you will see . . .' that is remarkable. Mark could not have shown Jesus prophesying that the High Priest and his company would see the coming of the Son of Man if he did not consider that in some sense it would happen within their lifetime. Clearly, he cannot have envisaged merely a coming at the end of time, for Mark wrote at least thirty years after this event. He must have been envisaging an event which had occurred before he wrote his gospel. This event can only have been the Resurrection itself or something connected with it. In some sense, therefore, one can only conclude that Mark envisaged the fulfilment of the kingdom as occurring at the Resurrection.

Jesus' view of the kingdom

It cannot be overstressed that here we are considering only Mark's view of the kingdom, not yet Jesus' own view. It is quite possible that these are genuine sayings of Jesus which Mark has put in these contexts, thereby giving them a specific application. It will be argued later that in fact the scene of the interrogation before the High Priest is a scene composed by the evangelist. It is not therefore evidence for Jesus' own view.

Jesus in the Temple

Perhaps most significant of all in understanding what is meant by the kingship of God is the popular cry at the Entry into Jerusalem, hailing 'the coming kingdom of David our father' (Mk 11:10). This must imply that the kingship of David, the messianic kingship, is in some way being fulfilled at Jesus' entry into the holy city for the final phase of his ministry. The great celebration, whose scriptural allusions are all instinct with messianic overtones, provides a patch of joyful light before the sombre events which follow. Does 'the coming kingdom' refer to the immediate event, the entry itself and Jesus' activity in the Temple, or to the climax of that short week, the Resurrection?

The meaning of Jesus' action in the Temple has been disputed. It is often seen as a mere cleansing of offensive practices, money changing and the sale of sacrificial victims. However, there is no indication that these activities were real abuses. Rates charged for changing the money for the coinage required in the Temple do not seem to have been excessive, and the sacrificial victims were needed for the Temple-worship itself. Furthermore, if Jesus had meant merely to cleanse abuses in the Temple practice, the most effective sign would have been water.

There is no doubt that this action of Jesus was the cause of the violent reaction of the Jerusalem authorities against Jesus, and their determination to do away with him. The Temple and its rites were the glory of Jerusalem.

According to the Roman natural historian Pliny the Elder, it was the Temple which made Jerusalem 'by far the most distinguished city of the East'. The disciples were right to wonder at the great stones, 'Master, look at the size of these stones' (Mk 13:1). The largest of them still remaining is 12 metres long and 3 metres by 4 metres in cross-section, and weighs 400 tonnes. In general the dimensions of it were staggering. The retaining wall of the esplanade on which it was built rose 30 metres above the street level. The royal portico on the south of the great esplanade was one and a half times the length of Salisbury Cathedral (186 metres compared to 137 metres). The ten great pairs of gilded gates were each 13 metres by 6.6 metres.[4] Its wealth was fabulous: the Roman general Crassus stole from it 2000 talents in cash, and there were gold vessels worth 8000 talents.[5] Above all, it was the goal of pilgrimage for Jews all over the Mediterranean area, the religious and cultural centre of the nation, served by some 20,000 priests.

Jesus' action in the Temple must be seen in connection with the accusation at his trial and the mockery on the Cross. He was accused of saying, 'I am going to destroy this Temple . . . and in three days build another, not made by human hands' (14:58). This saying is preserved also in a slightly different form in John 2:20. The Jewish leaders who mocked him on the Cross also referred to this claim, 'Aha! So you would destroy the Temple and rebuild it in three days!' (Mk 15:29). Jesus' action in the Temple was construed, then, as his attempt to destroy

[4] Josephus, *Bellum Judaicum*, 5.
[5] Josephus, *Antiquities*, 14:72; 105–9.

the Temple, a symbolic act of destruction, as part of his claim to build a new Temple.

The building of a new Temple was part of the hope of Israel for the last times. Ezekiel 40—44 is a complete blueprint for this renewed Temple, but the Temple is also a constant theme in other Jewish writings:

> My soul blesses the Lord, the great King
> because Jerusalem will be built anew
> and his house for ever and ever.   (Tb 13:15—16)

The complete meaning of this action in the Temple, then, can be seen only in the context of the final renewal of Israel and Jerusalem. Mark stresses this by sandwiching the account of the demonstration in the Temple between the two halves of the Barren Fig Tree; this little acted parable is symbolic of the barrenness of Israel and of the withering of the old order (11:12—14, 20—1). This gives the meaning of what Jesus was bringing about by his demonstration in the Temple. This was what the authorities were determined to prevent. They challenged his authority so to act, but received no reply beyond the hint that his authority was the same as that of John the Baptist, which popular acclaim pronounced to be divine authority (11:27—33). There was then no other way to keep their power secure than to liquidate Jesus.

4 BIBLIOGRAPHY

Chilton, B., (ed), *The Kingdom of God*, London, SPCK, 1984. See especially the essay by Michael Lattke, 'On the Jewish background of the synoptic concept "The Kingdom of God" '.

Dodd, C. H., *The Parables of the Kingdom*, London, Nisbet, 1936.

Dodd, C. H., *The Founder of Christianity*, London, Collins, 1976.

France, R. T., *Divine Government*, London, SPCK, 1991.

Meyer, Ben, *The Aims of Jesus*, London, SCM, 1979. See Chapters 6—9.

Neill, S., and Wright, N. T., *The Interpretation of the New Testament 1861–1986*, Oxford, Oxford University Press, 1988. See Index, under 'kingdom'.

Perrin, Norman, *The Kingdom of God in the Teaching of Jesus*, London, SCM, 1963.

Räisänen, Heikki, *The 'Messianic Secret' in Mark's Gospel*, Edinburgh, T. & T. Clark, 1990.

Sanders, E. P., *Jesus and Judaism*, London, SCM, 1985.

Sanders, E. P., *Judaism, Practice & Belief, 63 BCE to 66 CE*, London, SCM, 1992.

Schweitzer, Albert, *The Quest of the Historical Jesus*, tr. W. Montgomery, London, Black, 1961 (from German, *Von Reimarus zu Wrede*, 1906).

5 PERSONAL STUDY

Either write an essay, using only the Markan material, answering the question, 'In what sense does Jesus make present the kingship of God?' *or* discuss the statement, 'In Mark the Good News is the kingship of God'.

CHAPTER 6

WHAT DID MARK THINK OF JESUS?

As in the previous enquiry about the kingship of God, it is essential to distinguish between what Mark thought of Jesus and what Jesus thought of himself. Again, the two concepts must be in continuity, but with the deepening of understanding of the nature and significance of the life, death and resurrection of Jesus, and with the particular circumstances of Mark's community, different aspects may well come to the fore. To begin with, Mark's gospel is primarily concerned with the gradual revelation of who Jesus was, whereas, as Morna Hooker says, 'it is clear that for Jesus himself it was the proclamation of God's kingdom, not his own messianic status, that was central'.[1]

A second caution is also important. For Christians Jesus is the Word made flesh, the incarnate Son of God. This understanding of Jesus is, however, the product of centuries of deepening of understanding. 'Word', 'flesh' and 'incarnate' are terms which have no place in Mark, and 'Son of God' is an expression which can bear a variety of meanings in the Old Testament. Mark stands early in the Christian development of understanding of the Master, and it cannot be assumed that his view of Christ is in all respects explicitly the same as that of the Council of Nicaea, or even of the Gospel of John. It is an important point of departure to realise that Jesus never calls himself 'God'. Nowhere in Mark is Jesus called 'God'. Indeed, only three times in the New Testament is Jesus explicitly so called, and all of these instances stand at the very end of the process of development and reflection (Jn 1:1; 20:28; Heb 1:8). It is possible therefore, and indeed necessary, to ask how

[1] Morna Hooker, *The Gospel of Mark* p. 201.

Mark's Good News represents Jesus, and what it contributes to the deepening understanding of his role and being.

1 THE SHAPE OF THE GOSPEL

Mark's gospel is full of wonder, a wonder gradually focusing on the person of Christ. Like so many of his individual short phrases and expressions, as a whole it falls into two halves, pivoting on the episode at Caesarea Philippi: the first half is devoted to the gradual discovery that Jesus is the Christ, the Messiah, as Peter acknowledges for the first time on that occasion; the second half is devoted to the gradual and painful discovery of the nature of his messiahship, that it is the way of suffering and rejection.

The gospel is defined not only in the middle, but at both ends as well. The first section and the last are particularly significant. Although the gospel is a gradual process of wondering discovery, this amazement applies primarily to the actors in the drama, and especially to the disciples. To the reader the first section gives the game away. The introductory section is as true an introduction as the Prologue of John or the Infancy Stories of Matthew and Luke, for it sets the scene and informs the reader of the true nature and import of the story to come.

The prologue of Mark

The prologue to the gospel (1:1–13) sets the scene carefully. It falls into three sections: the testimony of tradition, the Baptism and the Testing of Jesus. But before that comes the heading, which is itself highly significant: 'The beginning of the gospel about Jesus Christ, the Son of God'.

These last three words are missing in some manuscripts, but are supremely apt. With the declaration of the centurion at the foot of the Cross, 'In truth this man was Son of God' (Mk 15:39), they bracket the gospel. In accordance with the ancient literary (and the modern mathematical) convention, this is a way of showing that everything within the bracket is defined and characterised by the bracket itself. In this case, therefore, that means the gospel is characterised as the gospel of the Son of God. This expression arches over the gospel, which consists in showing that and how Jesus is the Son of God.

The tradition

The testimony of tradition is given by the quotation from the prophets and by the preparation done by the Baptist. Both of these show that Jesus stands within the tradition, or rather as the climax of the tradition, of Israel. The prophets testify to him. The Baptist is clad as a prophet and especially as Elijah, who was the final prophet foretold by Malachi to be the immediate herald of the final coming of the Lord. Malachi 3:1 is even quoted in Mark 1:3. The quotation from Isaiah hints already that the coming of Jesus is the coming of the Lord. Isaiah 40:3 reads:

> A voices cries, 'Prepare in the desert
> a way for Yahweh.
> Make a straight highway for our God . . .'

Here the person for whom John prepares the way and makes a straight highway is Jesus; he has taken the place of 'Yahweh' and 'our God', so that his position is already hinted.

The Baptism

The central scene of the prologue is that of the Baptism of Jesus. Or rather, not so much the Baptism as the authentication of Jesus on the occasion of his Baptism. The authorisation of a rabbi, or the divine guarantee of a particular interpretation put forward by a rabbi, given by a voice from heaven, is a well-known convention of Jewish literature. So the basic point of the voice from heaven is to authorise Jesus' mission. In this particular case, however, there are three modalities of this authorisation which should be noted. They are implied by the words, 'You are my Son, the Beloved; my favour rests on you' (Mk 1:11).

First, the expression 'son of God' does not in itself by any means imply the incarnate Son of God, the Second Person of the Trinity. In the Old Testament it is not so exclusive a term. It is used to describe various people who are especially close to God, who stand in a special relationship to him and have a special mission from God for which he empowers them. Thus angels are called sons of God, Israel itself is called

God's son, and so are the judges and rulers of his people; latterly the Wisdom literature calls the just man 'God's son'.[2] Thus far in Mark its exact sense remains to be defined. But at least it denotes that Jesus is the chosen representative of God, with a special mission to perform. It suggests that in some sense he is the embodiment of the people of Israel.

Secondly, the words 'You are my Son' (as some manuscripts of Luke make clear by adding 'today have I fathered you', 3:22) are an allusion to Psalm 2:7. This psalm is the celebration of a royal coronation, in the tradition of the Egyptian court ceremonial. In this tradition, the king was held to be adopted by the god. Similarly in the Davidic tradition, the king is considered God's son. So these words of the voice from heaven imply the kingship of Jesus, and suggest that Jesus is the king-messiah of the line of David, a theme stressed by Mark in his narrative of the Trial and Crucifixion.

Thirdly, the phrase 'my favour rests on you' is an allusion to the Song of the Servant of the Lord in Isaiah 42:1. The second part of Isaiah contains four songs of a mysterious Servant of the Lord, who will suffer and die to save his people. This is the opening of the first song:

> Here is my servant whom I uphold,
> my chosen one on whom my favour rests.
> I have sent my spirit upon him,
> he will bring fair judgement to the nations.

The allusion is strengthened by the mention of the descent of the spirit of the Lord in Isaiah, echoed by the mention of the Spirit immediately afterwards in Mark 1:10. Integral to these songs is the suffering, persecution and redemptive death of the Servant, so that by identification with the Servant the suffering and death of Jesus are already introduced in this prologue itself. This quality of Jesus as the Servant of the Lord will be stressed again and again in the course of the gospel by allusions to the Songs of the Suffering Servant in Isaiah. In Mark 10:45 Jesus alludes to it by saying, 'The Son of man himself came not to be served but to serve, and to give his life as a ransom for many.'

Allusions to Isaiah

Here the expression $\psi v \chi \grave{\eta}$ $\alpha \grave{v} \tau o \hat{v}$ and $\pi o \lambda \lambda o \acute{\iota}$ ('his life' and 'many') are allusions to the Servant Song in Isaiah 53:10, and $\delta o \hat{v} v \alpha \iota$, $\acute{v} \pi \grave{\varepsilon} \varrho$ and $\lambda \acute{v} \tau \varrho o v$ ('to give', 'ransom' and 'for') to Isaiah 43:1–4.

---

[2] See *The New Jerusalem Bible*, Mt 4:3, note *d*.

In the account of the institution of the eucharist the new covenant recalls Isaiah 42:6, 'I have made you a covenant of the people and light to the nations', and a similar promise in Isaiah 49:8.

The Testing

The third element of the introduction is the Testing for forty days by Satan in the desert (1:12–13). This is an echo, made much more explicit in the accounts of Matthew and Luke, of the testing of God's son Israel for forty years in the desert. Where Israel failed, Jesus, God's son, remains faithful. But two further elements of Jesus' mission which will be prominent in the gospel are here presaged, the struggle with Satan which will occur in Jesus' expulsion of evil spirits, and his testing by suffering and persecution. Each of these will form a major theme in the gospel story.

The main thrust of the revelation of Jesus in the gospel is, then, already foreseen and suggested in these thirteen verses of prologue.

The conclusion of Mark

The conclusion of Mark (16:1–8) consists of the story of the Empty Tomb. This in its turn confirms the message which has already been adumbrated in the prologue.

Mark 6:9–20 appears to be the conclusion. It should not, however, be considered part of the original gospel of Mark, and so evidence of his theology. The manuscript tradition is complicated. In brief, two different additional endings are preserved in various manuscripts, neither of which is particularly strongly attested. The most likely solution is that once the gospels of Matthew and Luke had come into being, with their full stories of the appearances of the Risen Lord, it was felt that Mark was incomplete without any such stories. The 'longer ending' (vv. 9–20) can be seen at a glance to be a secondary collection of scraps drawn from sayings of the gospels and the Acts of the Apostles about the Resurrection Appearances and the future mission of the disciples, brief résumés of a quite different character from Mark's lively stories. It will be assumed in this book, without further argument but with the virtually unanimous agreement of scripture scholarship, that these verses should be left out of consideration in seeking Mark's own meaning.

In the early Christian tradition the Resurrection is considered to be the vital completion of the story of Jesus' death, without which it makes no sense. In particular his position as Lord is established by the Resurrection. To take only two examples, in the early hymn quoted by

Paul in Philippians 2:6–11, the Resurrection is the decisive moment when he receives the awesome name of Lord (which is seen by the quotation of Isaiah 45:23 to be the divine name):

And for this God raised him high,
and gave him the name
which is above all other names,
so that *all beings*
in the heavens, on earth and in the underworld,
should bend the knee at the name of Jesus
and that *every tongue should acknowledge*
Jesus Christ as Lord
to the glory of God the Father.   (Ph 2:9–10)

In the decisive prologue to Romans, similarly, the Resurrection is the moment of Jesus' establishment in power:

This is the gospel concerning his Son who, in terms of human nature was born a descendant of David and who, in terms of the Spirit and of holiness was designated Son of God in power by resurrection from the dead . . .   (Rm 1:3–4)

The message of Mark's story of the Empty Tomb is that, with Jesus' rising from the dead, divine power has entered human experience and human life in a quite new way. Almost all the elements of these eight verses concentrate on this. First Mark stresses the familiar theme of the incomprehension of Jesus' followers. The women have no idea of what is to happen. They are pretty muddled in any case! In Palestine to try to anoint a body two days after death is not a sensible proposition: decay will have set in. They think only too late that they will not, anyway, be able to gain access by rolling the stone away, 'for it was very great' (v. 4, a typical Markan afterthought-explanation introduced by *gar*, 'for' see p. 37).

The passage is not in any way a proof of the emptiness of the tomb nor a proof of the Resurrection. The young man in a white robe invites the women to check that the tomb is empty, 'See, here is the place where they laid him' (v. 6), but they make no attempt to do so. If the passage were intended to prove the reality of the disappearance of the body, it would have included a thorough examination of the empty tomb in order to confirm the angel's words. Instead, what is given is the explanation or interpretation of the fact, the fact itself being taken for granted. Providing such explanations is the function of an *angelus interpres* ('interpreting angel').

Interpreting angels

The convention of an *angelus interpres* would be immediately recognised from previous biblical and other Jewish literature. Such a young man is a stock figure to explain supernatural happenings (Ezk 40:3; Zc 1:9; 2:2, 7, etc.; Dn 8:15; 9:21–2; 2 M 3:33).

His function is confirmed by the reaction of the women when they see him: amazement. This is the stock reaction to a heavenly messenger, who then reassures them (vv. 5–6).

In a way the real meaning of the event becomes clear principally in the reaction of the women to the explanation: 'they were frightened out of their wits; and they said nothing to anyone, for they were afraid' (v. 8) – literally, 'Trembling and ecstasy gripped them . . . for they were afraid'.

The idea of resurrection was no new one in Judaism. Since Maccabean times, two centuries before Jesus, it had been normal to expect a general resurrection at the end of time. What was startling about this event was that the resurrection scheduled to come with the final visitation of God at the end of time, and accompanied by the ending of the present structure of the world, was suddenly seen to have occurred in Jesus' Resurrection. The final event had already occurred in Jesus. The awesome fact was that God had broken into world history. This was a shattering manifestation of the divine.

Awe and fear are the natural reaction to the divine, and here it is three times repeated, in characteristically Markan style, first with a Markan doublet ('trembling and ecstasy'), then with a typical Markan afterthought-explanation introduced by *gar*, 'for'. It is with this that the gospel comes to an end; the fear and awe of the women is left hanging in the air, leaving the gospel open-ended. The message is that at the Resurrection the divine has burst upon human history with all its awe-inspiring potential.

Thus the last scene of the gospel answers to the first, as Jesus' divine sonship is established in a new way and recognised at the Resurrection.

The Transfiguration

The same emphasis on Jesus' divine sonship occurs also at the turning point of the gospel. Immediately after the scene at Caesarea Philippi (Peter's confession, followed by the first prophecy of the Passion and its sequels (see page 42), Mk 8:27–38), the Transfiguration (9:2–8) again makes clear that Jesus is the authoritative Son of God, as the voice from the divine cloud reiterates and expands the words at the Baptism, 'This is my Son, the Beloved. Listen to him.' Numerous traits link this episode to the Resurrection, to the extent that it has been interpreted as a misplaced or anticipated Resurrection Narrative. The white garments and the transfiguring bespeak a heavenly being, as does the fear of the onlookers. The account is bracketed at either end by the statement that the kingdom of God is about to come in power (9:1) and the allusion to the Resurrection (9:9). This scene, then, acts as a reminder of the true nature of Jesus as the disciples begin to learn that he is to suffer as Messiah.

2 THE SON OF GOD IN ACTION

Within this careful framing by Mark there are four other features which bring out the special quality of Jesus: the constant wonder at his actions, his authority, the recognition by evil spirits, and the nature miracles.

The constant wonder of the witnesses to Jesus

An atmosphere of awe and wonder pervades the gospel, a feeling that Jesus is more than an ordinary human being. This is sometimes in reaction to his deeds, sometimes consequent upon what he does not do.

When he calls the first disciples, for example, they follow without question, no explanation being given or needed; they seem simply to be drawn by his personality (Mk 1:18, 20; 2:14). Luke modifies this to give some previous miracles which explain their response (Lk 5:1–11). When Jesus gives the disciples authority, they go off without question to execute his mission (Mk 6:7). When he sends the disciples to commandeer a mount, they depart without question and the owners respond without hesitation (11:1–6). Similarly (and indeed the two passages are closely paired, and deliberately reflect each other), when Jesus sends his disciples to order a room for the Last Supper, the owner again responds without hesitation or question (14:13–16).

His authority is remarkable: 'his teaching made a deep impression on them because, unlike the scribes, he taught with authority' (1:22). 'Here is a teaching that is new, and with authority behind it' (1:27). 'Even the wind and the sea obey him' (4:41), 'And after that no one dared to question him any more' (12:34). It is not only among the simple countryfolk that his unquestioning and unquestioned authority prevails. He commands always like one whose orders cannot be questioned. Questioners come to him, asking for decisions on all kinds of issues – fasting, the payment of tribute, the interpretation of scripture. On the occasion when his authority is challenged (11:27–33), he is not at all shaken, but leaves his challengers themselves confused and challenged.

His reputation spreads 'everywhere, through all the surrounding Galilean countryside' (1:28). 'Everybody is looking for you' (1:37); 'great numbers who had heard of all he was doing came to him' (3:8); 'wherever he went, to village or town or farm, they laid down the sick in the open spaces, begging him to let them touch even the fringe of his cloak' (6:56).

His miracles excite awe and astonishment: 'they were all astonished, and praised God saying, "We have never seen anything like this" ' (2:12). 'They were overcome with awe and said to one another, "Who can this be? . . ." ' (4:41). 'And everyone was amazed' (5:20). 'At once they were overcome with astonishment' (5:43). 'They were utterly and completely dumbfounded' (6:51). 'Their admiration was unbounded' (7:37). The awe and astonishment are, of course, at the cures worked by Jesus. But cures and wonderful healings were not unprecedented: there were examples known also at Greek shrines and among Hellenistic and Galilean charismatics. What is especially remarkable is the commanding way in which Jesus accomplishes these miracles. With rare exceptions there is none of the machinery common in other miracle stories, no impassioned prayer to God for a miracle, no spitting, no anointing, no abracadabra. The sick simply put their trust in Jesus and he responds.

The evidence sketched so far shows that Jesus' personality is remarkable; but as yet its source is unfocused.

Recognition by evil spirits

The initial conflict with Satan which concludes the introduction already suggests that the expulsion of unclean spirits by Jesus may have special importance. It is the unclean spirits who first acknowledge Jesus as 'the Holy One of God' (1:24) and 'son of the Most High God' (5:7). The fact that neither the disciples nor other onlookers seem to be affected or informed by these cries indicates that they are not intended to be taken as literal sayings, actually audible. It is more Mark's way of expressing the acknowledgement of Jesus' power evident in the return of the possessed man to normality. This return to normality is understood as an acknowledgement of Jesus as Son of God, expressed in the cry of

the unclean spirit. It is an indication of Mark's view of Christ, parallel
to the voice from heaven at the Baptism and the Transfiguration.

The nature miracles

Among the miracles of Jesus the two miracles of the sea stand out for
their symbolic value. The fear and awe of the disciples at the Calming
of the Storm are all the more remarkable as a contrast to their earlier
ironic sarcasm, 'Master, do you not care? We are lost!' (4:39). Their
change from cynicism to admiration can be explained against the background of Psalm 107:23–9:

> Voyagers on the sea in ships,
> plying their trade on the great ocean,
> have seen the works of Yahweh,
> his wonders in the deep.
>
> By his word he raised a storm-wind,
> lashing up towering waves.
> Up to the sky then down to the depths!
> Their stomachs were turned to water;
> they staggered and reeled like drunkards,
> and all their skill went under.
>
> They cried out to Yahweh in their distress,
> he rescued them from their plight,
> he reduced the storm to a calm,
> and all the waters subsided,
> and he brought them, overjoyed at the stillness,
> to the port where they were bound.

Jesus has taken the place and played the part of Yahweh. Similarly, in
the story of the Walking on the Water, Jesus is seen to play the part of
God, for it is only Yahweh who can walk on the sea:

> He and no other has stretched out the heavens
>   and trampled on the back of the Sea.   (Job 9:8)
>
> Your way led over the sea,
> your path over the countless waters,
> and none could trace your footsteps.   (Psalm 77:19)

Perhaps, as Morna Hooker suggests, there is a special significance in the
fact that this wonder immediately follows the miraculous Feeding of
the Five Thousand. The Feeding is carefully shaped by allusions to

bring out the lesson that Jesus is like Moses in providing bread for his people in the desert; in the succeeding story the allusions to God alone being in control of the sea show that he is still more than Moses. In the story of Israel's Exodus from Egypt, the manna in the desert and God leading his people across the sea occur one after the other. 'The crossing of the sea and the gift of manna are the central miracles in the Exodus story, and it is therefore not surprising to find Mark tying these two miracles of Jesus closely together'.[3]

3 THE SON OF MAN

A very frequent designation which Jesus uses for himself in Mark is 'the Son of man'. The derivation and original meaning of this expression have been hotly disputed. How Jesus originally intended it, what he meant by it, and whence it is derived, will be considered in a later chapter (see pages 100–1). In Mark, however, the meaning of it is less obscure. It occurs fourteen times in Mark, always on Jesus' own lips, and in two different ways.

Of Jesus' Passion, Death and Resurrection

Jesus uses the phrase several times in speaking of his approaching Passion, Death and Resurrection. It plays a key role in the three great prophecies of the Passion (8:31; 9:31; 10:33), again in another prophecy of the Passion and vindication (9:9, 12), and is used three times of the Passion without explicit mention of the Resurrection (10:45; 14:21, 41).

Of Jesus' authority

The other way in which the Markan Jesus uses this expression of himself is to state his authority. On two occasions this is his authority on earth, authority to forgive sins (2:10) and authority over the Sabbath (2:28). On the other occasions, all the sayings are in prominent positions, and therefore all the more important for Mark's view of Jesus.

> '. . . For if anyone in this sinful and adulterous generation is ashamed of me and of my words, the Son of man will also be ashamed of him when he comes in the glory of his Father with the holy angels.'   (8:38)

---

[3] Morna Hooker, *The Gospel of Mark*, p. 169.

This saying leads into the Transfiguration (see page 73), when Jesus is already seen in the glory which will be his. It is a presage of the final judgement.

> '. . . And then they will see the Son of man coming in the clouds with great power and glory. And then he will send the angels to gather his elect from the four winds . . .'   (13:26-7)

This is the climax of the 'eschatological discourse', the foretelling of the persecution of Jesus' community in the world, ending with their liberation by the Son of man (see page 45-6).

> '. . . you will see the Son of man seated at the right hand of the Power and coming with the clouds of heaven.'   (14:62)

The importance of this saying is that it forms the climax of the inter-rogation before the High Priest. In Mark's presentation it is the claim which constitutes the point of his final rejection by the Jewish authori-ties, and leads immediately to the decision to have him killed. The claim is judged by the High Priest and his council to be blasphemy. It is not immediately clear why this should be blasphemy – certainly the claim to be the Messiah is not blasphemous, for other messianic claim-ants soon before or after this were not condemned for blasphemy. Most probably the reason is the combination of 'seated at the right hand of the Power' and 'coming with the clouds of heaven'. This implies that Jesus is to be at the right hand of God on his throne. But if while 'seated' he is also 'coming', he must be actually sharing the mobile throne of God. This throne is the chariot-throne on which God is seated in Ezekiel 1. Already at the time of Jesus this imagery bulked large in the imagination and descriptions of Jewish mysticism (called Merkabah mysticism). Such a claim would give good grounds for the charge of blasphemy.

From these three key sayings it is clear that for Mark the background of the expression 'Son of man' is the prophecy of Daniel 7:13-14:

> I was gazing into the vision of the night,
> when I saw, coming on the clouds of heaven,
> as it were a son of man.
> He came to the One most venerable
> and was led into his presence.
> On him was conferred rule,
> honour and kingship,
> and all peoples, nations and languages became his servants.
> His rule is an everlasting rule

which will never pass away,
and his kingship will never come to an end.

In the prophecy preceding this vision Daniel describes four great beasts, representing the four great empires which persecuted and oppressed the Jewish nation. The 'son of man', in his turn, represents the nation itself, at last vindicated and triumphant, and finally to rule over the whole world with God's own authority. Mark understands the expression, well known to have been characteristic of Jesus, to designate this Son of man, sharing God's power and authority. However in this final saying he goes beyond the prophecy, to represent Jesus as sharing the throne itself of God. To those who did not accept Jesus, this would indeed be a blasphemy horrific in its audacity. The trial scene is, then, for Mark the climax of his presentation of the mystery and meaning of Jesus.

4 PERSONAL STUDY

1. Work through the articles in J. L. McKenzie's *Dictionary of the Bible* (London, Geoffrey Chapman, 1965), and the notes in *The New Jerusalem Bible* (see the Index of Footnotes in the 1994 edition) on 'Son of God' and 'Son of man'.
2. Write an essay entitled 'What does Mark mean by calling Jesus "Son of God"?' That is, write your own conclusions about this section!

CHAPTER 7

MARK'S PASSION NARRATIVE

The interests of the evangelists in presenting the story of Jesus were never merely historical. Mark's aim was to convey the sense and meaning of the events. There is no dwelling upon the gruesome sufferings which were intended by this hideous form of execution. The crucifixion itself is narrated in one short phrase, 'Then they crucified him' (Mk 15:24). There is no dwelling on the stripping or nailing or other incidents familiar from Christian piety. The factual details were all too familiar to contemporaries. The issue was more to interpret what had happened, to enable Christians to understand how their Lord and Master could have come to undergo this demeaning and disgraceful form of ultimate torture.

In this chapter we will consider first the political realities underlying the execution of Jesus, then the chief motifs behind the narration in Mark, and finally the individual incidents leading up to the crucifixion in Mark's narrative.

1 THE UNDERLYING POLITICAL REALITIES

The opposition to Jesus

A sharp distinction must be made between the opposition to Jesus during his Galilean ministry and the opposition he encountered in Jerusalem itself.

The disputes in Galilee between Jesus and the legal authorities, lawyers and those meticulous practitioners of the Law, the Pharisees, did not go beyond the bounds of acceptable legal dispute. Exactly how the Law should be observed, and how clashes between different values in the Law should be resolved, were everyday subjects of controversy at the time. Jesus' attitude and behaviour would have been highly irritating to the Pharisees, but not worthy of any death penalty. The series of controversies assembled by Mark in 2:1—3:6 culminate in a plot between the Pharisees and the Herodians, 'discussing how to destroy him'. Jesus had done nothing yet to justify such extreme hostility, and it may be that Mark is already looking ahead to the final outcome, and alerting the reader to this: the word used for 'plan' occurs only here and after Jesus' arrest, in 15:1.

In fact these disputes with Pharisees are not even represented as playing any part in the process which finally led to Jesus' execution. After 12:13 the Pharisees play no further part, but disappear totally from the scene. The Pharisees as such had no political power or voice. The local government, which continued to function under Roman oversight, was in the hands of the Sadducees, the priestly families, under the overall jurisdiction of the High Priest.

Contemporary codes of law

Little is known of the code of law under which the Sadducees operated. The Pharisaic code of law, which began to be developed during the regrouping after the Fall of Jerusalem in AD 70, was never the law of a state; it remained merely theoretical. In fact it is so hedged round with cautions and protections for the accused that it would scarcely have been operable. These attitudes displayed in the law code do, however, suggest that the Pharisees may have abstained from effective action against Jesus because they were too timid and too righteous to participate in any dubious legal proceedings.

The events leading up to Jesus' arrest focus on the Temple and the Temple authorities, the chief priests and Sadducees. They would have been the group chiefly affected by Jesus' demonstration in the Temple. If lawyers are mentioned, it is only in a subsidiary or supporting role. It is abundantly clear that the opposition from the Sadducees was sparked off by the demonstration in the Temple, by which Jesus made clear that he considered the Temple and its ritual to be obsolete and due for abolition. This lesson is, of course, pointed by Mark, when he sandwiches the incident between the prediction of the barrenness of the fig tree – a symbol of Israel – and its realisation. The Temple and its ritual were the glory of Jerusalem and the centre of pilgrimage for Jews from all over the Mediterranean region. A repeat of such a demonstration over Passover, when the city was thronged with pilgrims, would have been distasteful, insulting and politically destabilising; the authorities were taking no risks!

Two further factors point to the decisive importance of this event. Firstly, it is in this connection that the authorities challenge Jesus' authority (11:27–33). In rabbinic terms their question concerns the chain of authority: authority to teach came to a rabbi from another rabbi, his master. They ask this disruptive and authoritative figure from Galilee what his chain of authority is, only to receive the characteristic reply that it is outside their ken. If they accept only such chain-authority, they will refuse to accept his authority, just as they refused to accept John the Baptist's. Again the lesson is pointed by Mark, who follows this incident with the second of his two long parable stories in the gospel, the Wicked Tenants (12:1–9), declaring the bankruptcy of the current leadership of Israel.

Secondly, one of the best-remembered sayings of Jesus is the saying on the destruction and renewal of the Temple. This is cited at the hearing before the High Priest, as false evidence (but see page 89), 'We heard him say, "I am going to destroy this Temple made by human hands, and in three days build another, not made by human hands"' (14:58). It is the substance also of the gibe against Jesus on the Cross, 'Aha! So you would destroy the Temple and rebuild it in three days!' (15:29). In the Johannine version of the demonstration in the Temple Jesus himself says, 'Destroy this Temple, and in three days I will raise it up' (Jn 2:19). Finally, in the accusations against Stephen in the Acts of the Apostles, the same charge is repeated, 'We have heard him say that Jesus, this Nazarene, is going to destroy this Place' (Ac 6:13). If any trust may be put in this multiple attestation, it is plain that Jesus' saying rankled and bulked large in the minds of the Jerusalem authorities.

If Jesus' action was not enough of itself to provoke the Temple authorities, the opposition to the Temple from the sectaries at Qumran would have made them additionally sensitive. The writers of the Scrolls of Qumran had withdrawn into the desert out of opposition to the Temple and its rites. They reckoned that the Temple must be destroyed, and held that the new Temple which would replace it would consist of a renewed community:

> When these things come to pass in Israel,
> the Council of the Community shall be established in truth.
> It is a House of holiness for Israel . . .
> It is the tried wall, the precious corner-stone,
> its foundations shall not tremble.   (1 QS 8:5–8)

This threat from Qumran would have made the meaning of Jesus' action immediately apparent. Whatever occurred subsequently, therefore, was no more than the consequence of this incident in the Temple and the message it conveyed to the Temple authorities.

The judicial process

It was standard procedure in the Roman empire that provincial courts lacked the right to pass the death sentence. Roman provincial government used a combination of local and Roman jurisdiction, for they realised that on the whole locals could best govern their own people. The Roman governor of each province had three principal roles:

1. to maintain defence of the province and internal peace;
2. to judge cases of appeal, legal cases between cities or cases involving Roman citizens in the province;
3. to ensure the collection of taxes.

Most legal cases were judged by the local courts, but Romans reserved the death sentence to themselves, no doubt because it could otherwise be used to liquidate political opponents, and especially those disliked by the locals for supporting Rome too vigorously. John confirms that this was the case in Judaea when he has the Jews say to Pilate, 'We are not allowed to put a man to death' (Jn 18:31).

It was therefore necessary for the Jerusalem authorities to bring before the governor a charge which would appear to him to merit the death sentence. A charge which might seem to a Roman governor merely religious would not serve their purpose. When the Jews in Corinth were upset by Paul and arraigned him before the governor, they made precisely this mistake, with the result that the case was thrown out: 'Listen, you Jews. If this were a misdemeanour or a crime, it would be in order for me to listen to your plea; but if it is only quibbles about words and names, and about your own Law, then you must deal with it yourselves – I have no intention of making legal decisions about these things', said the governor (Ac 18:14–15). In consequence the president of the synagogue was set upon by his own people for his incompetence. The wily high priesthood of Jerusalem was far too experienced to be caught out like this. They would know how to present an effective charge to Pilate.

Pilate

Pilate has had a bad press from the Jewish historical sources, chief among whom are Josephus and Philo. Josephus was writing after the First Jewish Revolt, one of his two principal works being a history of that revolt (in which he himself had been a general on the Jewish side, had been captured, and had then worked on the Roman side). In defence of himself and his fellow-countrymen it was in his interests to show that the Jews, a people naturally peaceable and easily governed, were goaded to revolt by conduct on the part of Roman governors which it was beyond even the most placid human nature to endure. Pilate, one of the longest-serving of the governors (AD 26–36), is represented as a monster. He was eventually sent to Rome in 36 by his superior, the governor of Syria, after accusations of suppressing a messianic revolt in Samaria too brutally. He never returned. But this cannot be taken as evidence that his superiors condemned him for overreacting. It is possible that his governorship was terminated either because of the change of emperor which occurred at that moment, or because it was already long overdue to end. The way his office came to an end certainly cannot be taken as proof of his cruelty.

But it is possible to discern, beneath the propaganda of Philo and Josephus, that, rather than being a cruel monster, he was a well-intentioned and puzzled muddler, quite unable to cope with the Jewish skill in playing the trump card of their religious susceptibilities. The most recent assessment of Pilate (by B. C. McGing, in *Catholic Biblical Quarterly* **53** (1991), 417–38) represents his long rule as a period of comparative tranquillity and co-operation between the Jews and the Roman governor. Pilate seems to have done his best to work with the Jews, and on several occasions showed himself eventually willing to yield to pressure from the Jews. In the case of Jesus it is therefore quite likely that Pilate, reckoning him to be strictly innocent of the charges, yielded to the presumption that the Jews knew better and to their personal pressure on himself: 'If you set him free, you are no friend of Caesar's' (Jn 19:12).

The most obvious charge for the Jerusalem leaders to present was that of claiming to be the Messiah. The political overtones of the title at this time were perhaps the reason why Jesus was so careful not to encourage it. Obviously his actions and miracles could be represented as messianic. Especially the demonstration in the Temple could be seen as symbolic of a messianic renewal of Judaism. Although no earlier messianic revolt is yet known during Pilate's period of office, they had been endemic in Judaea since the death of Herod the Great (especially 4 BC and AD 6, and became so increasingly from AD 36 onwards). It is clear from Mark's accounts of both the Jewish hearing and the Roman trial that both in fact revolve round the accusation of claiming to be the Messiah. This is also the implication of the gibe to Jesus on the Cross, addressing him as 'the Christ, the King of Israel' (Mk 15:32). We may assume that this was the charge on which Jesus was condemned.

2 THE MOTIFS OF MARK'S NARRATIVE

God's will in scripture

In seeking to explain the distressing events of the execution of Jesus, Mark looks to the scriptures: it was bound so to happen, because it was already foretold as God's will in the predictions of scripture. Jesus himself explains his arrest as the fulfilment of scripture (14:49). The allusions to scripture become increasingly frequent as the death of Jesus itself approaches. The two chief texts on which the Passion story draws are Psalm 22 and Isaiah 53.

Psalm 22

The allusions to Psalm 22 are in the sharing out of his clothing (Mk 15:24, cf. Ps. 22:18); the jeers of the passers-by, and their shaking their heads (15:29, cf. Ps. 22:7); Jesus' final cry (15:34, cf. Ps. 22:1), and his thirst (15:36, cf. Ps. 22:15).

Isaiah 53

The silence of Jesus at the Jewish hearing and before Pilate (Mk 14:60–1) and 15:4–5) is probably seen as fulfilling the Song of the Suffering Servant (Is 53:7):

> like a lamb led to the slaughter-house,
> like a sheep dumb before its shearers
> he never opened his mouth.

Similarly the spitting in the mockery (Mk 14:65; 15:19) may well be echoes of the Servant Song (Is 50:6). These allusions follow the line of the sayings of Jesus. When he says that 'the Son of man himself came . . . to give his life as a ransom for many' (Mk 10:45), this may well be an allusion to Isaiah 53:10, 'he gives his life as a sin offering'. At the Last Supper the word over the cup, 'poured out for many' (Mk 14:24) similarly is an allusion to Isaiah 53:11, 'my servant will justify many by taking their guilt on himself'.

Other psalms

There are also many other allusions, such as the false witnesses who 'stood up' at the Jewish hearing (14:56–7);

> False witnesses have risen against me
> and are breathing out violence.   (Ps 27:12)

> False witnesses come forward against me
>   asking me questions I cannot answer,
> they cross-examine me, repay my kindness with cruelty,
>   make my life barren. (Ps 35:11)

As we have seen, the witness they bring about the Temple saying of Jesus does seem to be substantially accurate. Their falsity may well be seen to consist in their motivation in persecuting the Just One.

Another tiny allusion may be Peter standing 'at a distance' (14:54), the same word as in Psalm 38:11, 'Friends and companions . . . keep their distance.'

Amos

When there is darkness over the whole land from noon until the ninth hour (15:33), this should be seen as a fulfilment of Amos 8:9:

> On that Day – declares the Lord Yahweh –
> I shall make the sun go down at noon
> and darken the earth in broad daylight.

The evangelist is not describing a strange natural phenomenon unknown to astronomers, but is announcing that the Crucifixion of Jesus was the moment of the fulfilment of the Day of the Lord prophesied by Amos.

The foreknowledge of Jesus

Throughout Mark's gospel it is stressed that Jesus offered himself willingly and with full knowledge. Already in the first group of controversies he speaks of the bridegroom being taken away (Mk 2:20), and it may be assumed that he is aware of the plots even now to destroy him (3:6). In the three great prophecies of the Passion his predictions become ever more explicit (8:31; 9:31; 10:33).

The parable of the Wicked Tenants conveys a clear indication of Jesus' awareness that the leaders will do away with 'the son' (12:7–8). Even if this allegorical element is not original in the mind of Jesus, it is clear in Mark. Moreover, Jesus must, even humanly speaking, have been conscious that he had set himself on a collision course with the authorities of the Temple. As the time for the Passion approaches there is first the Anointing at Bethany, when he says that the woman 'has anointed my body beforehand for its burial' (14:8).

At the Last Supper the atmosphere is heavy with the approaching Passion. The passage on the treachery of Judas (14:17–21) in Mark is not primarily intended – as it is in Matthew – to point out the identity of the traitor; rather it underlines the depth of the betrayal by a friend who shares both table and dish. Jesus' saying over the cup reinforces this willing foreknowledge by allusion to the Song of the Suffering Servant. Most explicitly of all, Jesus' willingness is seen by his prayer of acceptance at the Agony in the Garden (14:36, 39), and by his calm greeting to Judas.

Throughout the gospel, then, Jesus is seen to expect and to accept his death, himself interpreting it by the prophecy of the Suffering Servant of Isaiah.

3 THE INDIVIDUAL UNITS OF THE PASSION STORY

It has often been held that the Passion story was handed down as a single unit from an early stage in the oral tradition, and that this was simply taken over by Mark with no more than slight modifications to stress the lessons of his theology. More and more, however, it has become clear that the narrative is shot through with his own procedure and style as well as with the theological motifs which have characterised the gospel as a whole. The obvious conclusion is that Mark was the first to put the oral tradition of the Passion Narrative into a written form, just as he was the first to put into written form the oral tradition of the gospel as a whole.

There must have been an accepted outline of the Passion story. The synoptic gospels all share the same detailed outline, stemming from Mark (though with some differences, particularly in Luke's account). John's account of the Passion is the most different from Mark's. It is independent of Mark's, and yet has a similar outline to Mark's, though with some striking differences. This similarity-with-difference is of just the kind which suggests a received pattern which underlay the gospel account before anything was written down either by Mark or by John.

1. John has no Agony in the Garden, though he gives a similar prayer (Jn 12:27).
2. Instead of Mark's hearing before the Sanhedrin presided over by the reigning High Priest, Caiaphas, John has a private interrogation before the ex-High Priest, Annas (Jn 18:13).
3. John's version of the hearing before Pilate (Jn 18:28–19:16) is largely different (and highly stylised). It has no mention of Barabbas. It is centred on the crowning of Jesus and the self-condemnation of the Jewish leaders before Jesus as judge.
4. John's account of the Crucifixion (Jn 19:17–30) itself runs quite a

different course. Jesus is in complete control of his destiny, and commits his mother and the Beloved Disciple to each other.

The Agony in the Garden

Mark must have used the same oral tradition of Jesus' prayer to his Father before the Passion as that which underlies John 12:27. (The Markan stylistic and theological characteristics are discussed on pages 34–7). He has shaped the scene to point the contrast between Jesus' steadfast and courageous acceptance of the Father's will and the slackness of the disciples. Even the faithful inner trio, Peter, James and John, who were with him at the Transfiguration (Mk 9:2), having been invited to share his prayer, fail to participate in any way. And at least Peter and James were to play a crucial role in the early Church.

In the scene of the arrest of Jesus this interplay between Jesus' steadfastness and the failure of the disciples continues. The disciple Judas left his Master at the supper with a sign of friendship, and now returns to betray him with another sign of friendship. The whole unit, 14:17–52, could be regarded as an extended Markan sandwich, bracketed by Judas' two acts of betrayal. Judas, 'one of the Twelve' (Mk 14:43), betrays Jesus with the very same sign of friendship, at the same time protesting that Jesus is his 'Rabbi' (a title used in Mark only by those who commit themselves to Jesus; others call him 'Teacher'). This is the last we see of the disciples: to a man they flee ('all of them', put by Mark in an emphatic position). To conclude the scene a young man who was trying to follow Jesus subjects himself to the spine-chilling humiliation of fleeing away naked.[1] He left all to flee from Jesus, as the disciples

---

[1] It may not be out of place to stress the horror of this. Modern translations happily use the expression 'naked' in such phrases as 'clothe the naked', which might suggest that lots of people wandered round Palestine without any clothes on. In fact the confusion is caused by Greek having a single word, γυμνος, to cover meanings which include 'unclad' and 'insufficiently/lightly clad'. The Jews had a special horror of nakedness.

earlier left all to follow him (10:28). This also fulfils the prophecy of Amos 2:16 for the Day of the Lord, 'On that day even the bravest of warriors will run away naked' (my translation).

The hearing before the High Priest

The historical content of this scene, in the oral tradition which lies behind Mark, is difficult to establish. The Johannine scene is very different, even in the matter of the chief interrogator, Annas rather than Mark's Caiaphas. The Sanhedrin may well have become more formal and prominent in Mark's narrative than it actually was at the time. There is no evidence that a Sanhedrin had any formal structure in Jesus' time. At the end of a long discussion E. P. Sanders writes, 'The evidence does not permit a firm decision about the existence of a supreme court with a fixed and known membership'.[2] More likely, rulers would assemble a body of supporters to reinforce their decisions. This is in fact the supportive role which the Sanhedrin plays in Mark's story of the trials.

On the unrolling of the trial J. Donahue wrote, 'Mark is the creator of the final form of the trial narrative. He takes over a tradition of an appearance of Jesus before a Jewish official, and merges this with a Christian apologetic of Jesus as the suffering Just One'.[3] Elsewhere he wrote, 'While Mark is anxious to creative a narrative which has the formalities of a trial, the technicalities and fine points of Jewish legal procedure are outside his main concerns'.[4] The interest of the scene is overwhelmingly theological: it is the climax of the rejection of Jesus.

This is conveyed by narrative. The outline pattern is Markan in several ways:

1. The Markan sandwich which contrasts Jesus' steadfastness with Peter's betrayal (see page 34).
2. Peter's triple denial and the triple accusation against Jesus (see page 36) is again a Markan construction. It is worth noting that the crescendo of denials follows a rabbinic schema: according to the rabbis, evasion is less grave than outright denial, and private denial less grave than public. Peter's denials increase in both these ways: the first is an evasion and to a single person; the second is a public

---

[2] E. P. Sanders, *Judaism, Practice and Belief, 63 BCE to 66 CE* (London, SCM, 1992), p. 488.

[3] In Werner H. Kelber (ed.), *The Passion in Mark* (Philadelphia, 1976), p. 78.

[4] J. Donahue, *'Are You the Christ?' The Trial Narrative in the Gospel of Mark* [SBLDS 10] (Missoula, 1973), p. 101.

repetition of the evasion; and the third is a public denial on oath. Thus Jesus stands up to the highest authority in Judaism, while Peter crumbles at the slightest threat, finally denying on oath any link with Jesus, when challenged by a mere slip of a girl.

3. There is a similarity in form between the Jewish hearing and the hearing before Pilate. The parallelism is expressed so carefully that it must reflect the author's mode of composition:

14:53 'They led Jesus off to the high priest'	15:1 'They . . . took [Jesus] away . . . to Pilate'
55 '. . . the whole Sanhedrin'	
53 The chief priests sought evidence without success	1 '. . . the rest of the Sanhedrin'
60 The High Priest addressed Jesus	3 the chief priests accused him without result
61 Jesus made no answer to evidence against him: 'he . . . made no answer at all'	4 Pilate addressed Jesus
	5 Jesus made no answer to accusations against him: 'Jesus made no further reply'
61 'The high priest put a second question', 'Are you the Christ . . .?'	2 'Pilate put to him this question', 'Are you the king of the Jews?'
62 Jesus answered, 'I am.'	Jesus answered, 'It is you who say it.'

4. The false accusers who occur in almost identical terms in 14:56 and 57–9 ('Several, indeed, brought false witness against him, but their evidence was conflicting'; 'Some stood up and submitted this false evidence against him . . . But . . . their evidence was conflicting') are expressed in such a way as to recall the false witnesses of the psalms against the Just One.

Enshrined in this framework, which has been so carefully devised by Mark, there are the two important accusations and Jesus' answer. The first accusation, the attempt to fasten on Jesus the Temple saying, shows that Mark appreciates the political issues which were at stake: if Jesus had indeed made such a threat against the Temple, he must be removed. The prominence throughout the Passion story of this accusation about the Temple increases the probability that Jesus' action in the Temple gave the final thrust which led to his arrest.

The second accusation and its answer are still more important for Mark's view of Jesus. The High Priest's question, 'Are you the Christ, the Son of the Blessed One?' (14:61), is not a traditional formulation. Nowhere in the Old Testament does this expression, 'Son of the Blessed One', occur; it would sound odd in the mouth of the High Priest, and may well be Mark's own interpretation of the title 'Christ' or 'Messiah', standing for the more traditional 'Son of God'. In any case, here again we find occurring the title 'Son of God' which Mark has used at important turning points of his gospel (see pages 68–71). In Jesus' reply to the High Priest we see most fully Mark's understanding of that title (see pages 74–5) whatever the political and juridical background, in Mark's gospel this is the claim for which Jesus goes to his death.

Thus, the scene as Mark presents it may well be a construction (by Mark, or possibly by the tradition on which he drew) to highlight the two reasons which led to Jesus' arrest and condemnation. In John there is no such meeting of the Sanhedrin after Jesus' arrest, only a private interrogation by Annas about Jesus' teaching. This is not to deny that at some time there was a meeting of the Sanhedrin to discuss the menace of Jesus, nor that these were in fact the reasons for which Jesus was sent to his death. In John, however, the decision by the Sanhedrin to liquidate Jesus is taken some time earlier (Jn 11:47). Raymond Brown comments,[5] 'A form of the Messiah question and answer was presented in the tradition as leading to Jesus' death . . . There is no uniformity in the existing Gospels as to whether the Messiah/Son of God/blasphemy issue was formally part of the Sanhedrin session that decided to put Jesus to death or was part of the atmosphere that contributed to the felt need to call a Sanhedrin to deal with Jesus.'

Jesus before Pilate

The historical basis

The amnesty at the Passover, which plays such an important part in this incident, is not elsewhere attested. However, since the Passover was the feast of the liberation of Israel from imprisonment in the House of Bondage, there would have been a certain aptness in this gesture of magnanimity. In any case, it serves to introduce the contrast between Jesus and Barabbas.

The scene is centred on the accusations brought by the chief priests and the title of 'king'. To gain the desired reaction from Pilate, the Jewish leaders would have so translated the title 'Christ', established at

[5] Raymond Brown, *The Death of the Messiah* (London, Geoffrey Chapman, 1994), p. 558.

the previous hearing. It is awkwardly introduced, for Pilate is first seen putting the title to Jesus, without any accusation having been made (15:2), and the reader is left to assume that the Jewish leaders have so accused Jesus. Mark clearly realises that the title will come as no surprise to the reader of his gospel. It is notable, also, that the title is phrased politically, 'king of the Jews', whereas the religious title would have been 'king of Israel'; the Jewish leaders are phrasing their accusation in such a way that Pilate cannot miss its political import.

The Markan scene

The outline of the scene is typically Markan. The process of questioning corresponds minutely to the process of the hearing before the Jewish authorities. But in the matter of legal detail the hearing before Pilate is just as unsatisfactory as the Jewish hearing. There is no sentence or condemnation; Pilate's only reaction to the charges against Jesus and his reply is wonder at Jesus' silence (15:5). Would it have been open to Pilate simply to dismiss Jesus? Instead Mark, by Pilate's triple question, emphasises where the true blame lies:

- 'Do you want me to release for you the king of the Jews?' (15:9)
- 'what am I to do with the man you call king of the Jews?' (15:12)
- 'What harm has he done?' (15:14)

The style is characteristically Markan throughout, but perhaps most tellingly in v. 10, 'For he realised it was out of jealousy that the chief priests had handed Jesus over' (a typical Markan afterthought-explanation, introduced by *gar*, 'for', and supplying the motivation of the characters in the drama). How decisive Mark feels this to have been is shown in his insistence that the chief priests had stirred up the crowd (15:11). Historically there was no obvious need for this: it was only to be expected that the Jerusalem crowd would reject this unknown figure from Galilee in favour of a rebel leader, imprisoned in Jerusalem, no doubt for a popular uprising which had occurred there. If they knew anything about Jesus, it would no doubt be only that he had mounted a demonstration against the Temple – not the way to gain popularity in a city where the Temple was the chief glory and the chief employer. Mark again stresses the insistence of the Jews, the crowd as well as the leaders, by his final motivation of Pilate, 'anxious to placate the crowd' (15:15).

The mockery

Both mockery and scourging are placed by John in the middle of the investigation by Pilate, by Mark after Pilate has given permission for execution. Benoit points out[6] that the scourging would have occurred later, as a preliminary to the execution itself; and that there would in reality have been other opportunities during the night for mockery by the soldiers during the delays in the investigation. For Mark, however, this 'burlesque of a coronation'[7] is most suitably placed here, as an ironical confirmation of Jesus' real kingship. Once again, the reader (knowing that the outcome was the Resurrection) sees a level of which the actors (who think that this is Jesus' last scene) are quite unaware. The irony, of course, is double:

- that the soldiers think they are mocking him, when in fact they are declaring what is really the case; and
- that the Jews deny his kingship, while the Romans recognise it.

The mockery goes beyond mere recognition as king. At this time in the Eastern empire, and increasingly at Rome itself also, a king was worshipped as divine. They offer Jesus *proskunesis*, which is properly the worship or prostration attributed to a divinity.

The crown might well reinforce this impression: the word used for 'thorn' would admit of long spikes which might suggest the sun-like rays of the crown of a divine king in the East. So the moment when his execution begins is also the moment when Jesus' full grandeur begins to be recognised.

The Crucifixion

Mark's account of the crucifixion and death of Jesus on the Cross is dominated by three themes; the fulfilment of scripture, the ironical recognition of Jesus as king and Son of God, and the breaking open of Judaism to admit gentiles also to the promises.

The fulfilment of scripture
The fulfilment of scripture has been prominent throughout the Passion Narrative (see pages 85–6); but in the final incident it becomes so important that there are few details which cannot be seen in this light.

---

[6] Pierre Benoit *The Passion and Resurrection of Jesus Christ* (tr. B. Weatherhead, New York, Herder and Herder 1969).

[7] Jerry Camery-Hoggatt, *Irony in Mark's Gospel* [Society of New Testament Studies Monograph Series 72] (Cambridge, CUP, 1992), p. 166.

This has provoked commentators to fruitless guesses about whether the early tradition would or would not have been likely to invent such detailed correspondences. More important is the fact that Mark, and behind him his community, saw one important aspect of the meaning of the Crucifixion in this exact fulfilment.

1. The offer of myrrhed wine (Mk 15:23) fulfils Proverbs 31:6:

> Procure strong drink for someone about to die,
>   wine for him whose heart is heavy:
> let him drink and forget his misfortune

2. The division of his clothing (Mk 15:24) fulfils Psalm 22:18:
>   they divide my garments among them
>   and cast lots for my clothing.

3. The two companions (Mk 15:27) fulfil Isaiah 53:12:

>   being counted as one of the rebellious

4. The jeering and wagging of heads (Mk 15:29) fulfils Psalm 22:7:

>   all who see me jeer at me,
>   they sneer and wag their heads

5. 'Aha!' (Mk 15:29) fulfils such psalms as Psalm 40:15 (cf. Ps 35:21; 70:3):

>   Let them be aghast with shame,
>   those who say to me, 'Aha, aha!'

6. Jesus' cry (Mk 15:34) fulfils Psalm 22:1:

>   My God, my God, why have you forsaken me?

7. The drink of vinegar (Mk 15:36) fulfils Psalm 69:21:

>   To eat they gave me poison,
>   to drink, vinegar when I was thirsty.

The two chief texts, Psalm 22 and Isaiah 53, must be seen as giving the sense of the event: both lead through suffering and rejection to the vindication of the sufferer, the salvation of his people, and the triumph of God.

Recognition as king and Son of God

In the body of the gospel the only kingship mentioned has been the kingship of God. From the scene of the hearing before Pilate onwards, the character of Jesus as king has suddenly come to the fore. Pilate himself asked Jesus (Mk 15:2) whether he was king of the Jews. With deliberate irony the soldiers mocked him as king (15:16–20). Now the placard on the cross stating the charge on which he is being executed proclaims him king of the Jews (15:26), and the passers-by increase the irony by mocking him as king. The chief priests and the scribes use not the political title 'king of the Jews' but the correct religious title 'king of Israel' (15:31–2). So only now on the Cross is his kingship of Israel recognised. The mockers themselves do not, of course, recognise it; no more do they really recognise that he 'saved others' in the sense in which the reader understands it. But the reader, who appreciates the irony of their mockery and the perfect ability of Jesus to come down from the cross and save himself, is reminded of his true kingship.

The ultimate climax, however, comes at the moment of the death of Jesus. It is then that, precisely in seeing how he had died, the centurion becomes the first human being to proclaim him as 'Son of God'. In the course of the gospel the voice from heaven has so named him, as have the unclean spirits, but never a human being.

This event must therefore be linked on the one hand to Paul's claim that he was 'designated Son of God in power by resurrection from the dead' (Rm 1:4), and on the other to the series of statements by Jesus indicating that the kingship of God is about to be fulfilled (see pages 62–3). These are indications that in some way this is the accomplishment of that hope.

The opening to the gentiles

Two details link the scene of the death of Jesus to that of the demonstration in the Temple. These two scenes answer to each other and illustrate each other. The meaning of the former scene was that the Temple ritual is now obsolete. An aspect of Jesus' teaching then underlined was, 'Does not scripture say: *My house will be called a house of prayer for all peoples*?' (Mk 11:17). One limitation of the Temple cult, therefore, was its restriction to Israel.

Now, immediately the gentile centurion acknowledges Jesus as Son of God, the obsolescence of the Temple is confirmed by the splitting of the veil of the Temple. The combined symbolism of these two events is either that the Temple is no longer a religious entity or that there is now access through the veil to the Holy of Holies for all nations – negative and positive sides of the same coin. The mission to the gentiles has begun.

4   BIBLIOGRAPHY

Benoit, Pierre, *The Passion and Resurrection of Jesus Christ*, tr. B. Weatherhead, New York, Herder and Herder, 1969.

Brown, Raymond E. *The Death of the Messiah*, London, Geoffrey Chapman, 1994.

Donahue, J., *'Are You the Christ?' The Trial Narrative in the Gospel of Mark* [SBLDS10], Missoula, Scholars Press, 1973.

Kelber, Werner H. (ed.), *The Passion in Mark*, Philadelphia, Fortress, 1976.

Senior, Donald, *The Passion of Jesus in the Gospel of Mark*, Wilmington, Michael Glazier, 1984.

5   PERSONAL STUDY

1. In Mark's Passion Narrative, search out and note:
   (a) all Old Testament allusions (use the marginal references given in a study Bible);
   (b) occurrences of 'king', 'Christ', 'messiah'.
2. Write an essay: 'How does Mark intend the reader to view the Passion and death of Jesus?'

CHAPTER 8

WHAT CAN WE KNOW ABOUT JESUS?

1 MARK'S VIEW OF CHRIST

Throughout this book the discussions have always been about Mark's view of things – Mark's view of the kingship of God, how Mark sees Jesus, how Mark presents the Passion and death of Jesus. Finally we must ask the important question about the relationship of Mark's view to the historical facts.

Obviously Mark's picture gives us direct access only to Mark's presentation, not to the historical facts. If Mark's gospel were a fictional work, this presentation would not have any necessary relationship to historical facts, beyond a general background of the period. If it were a 'documentary' (after the manner of television documentaries), it would nevertheless select some material, reject other material, and link together and 'angle' the selected material in such a way as to paint the picture as the deviser of the documentary saw it. Even with photography and newsreel, we are at the mercy of those who photograph and edit the material. The most one can hope for is a fair presentation of the facts. The discerning viewer will perhaps be able to criticise the presentation and see behind it to a truer view of the historical facts.

Granted that the gospel is a presentation of the Good News of Jesus Christ, two opposing attitudes are possible. The first is that of some fundamentalists. According to this attitude, only the proven words of Jesus and the record of the brute facts are of interest to those who follow him. It is important to amputate any words put into his mouth by others, to see through the biblical allusions and imagery in order to recapture what actually happened. At the Transfiguration, for instance, the clothes of Jesus actually turned white and a voice did sound in such a way that the words could have been captured on tape; only such words and such facts – and, of course, their meaning – are of interest to Christians.

The second attitude is that of those who value living tradition. The New Testament in general, and the gospels in particular, are the embodiment of the tradition of the first and most important generation of Christians. They form the foundation documents of the Church and are normative for all subsequent tradition. Their understanding of the Christ-event is therefore not only reliable but in its way certainly no less important than the brute facts themselves. If the words of Jesus have been expanded and applied, this expansion and application occurred under the guidance of the Spirit which guided the Church, and is itself therefore normative for Christians. If the deeds of Jesus are described by means of biblical allusion, this understanding of the events is more important than the 'brute' facts themselves – even if such 'brute' facts were recoverable. Which is more important, the colour of Jesus' clothes and the decibel-levels of sound, or the experience of Jesus undergone by the disciples? In this case, which are the 'brute' facts? How else can such experiences be described than by means of allusion and imagery ('Bottom falls out of stock market', 'England faces defeat')?

Fact and interpretation

The mathematician and philosopher Lewis Carroll poses the problem in *Alice in Wonderland* (Chapter 7):

> 'All right,' said the [Cheshire] Cat; and this time it vanished slowly, beginning with the end of the tail, and ending with the grin, which remained some time after the rest of it had gone.
>   'Well! I've often seen a cat without a grin,' thought Alice; 'but a grin without a cat! It's the most curious thing I ever saw in all my life!'

The logical nonsense occurs because the grin is a certain configuration of the cat, and cannot exist without what is configured. Or rather, to make matters worse, it is an interpretation of that configuration. In the same way, at the Transfiguration there must have been something which was described in the way it was described. The basic fact was the experience of Jesus which the chosen disciples had.

At this level it is valuable to the Christian to recover Mark's vision of Christ expressed in his version of the Good News, because he is the authorised messenger and evangelist of the Church. It will be valuable also to round out the picture by the study of the Good News according to Matthew, according to Luke, according to John, and according to Paul – different aspects of the same prism, as St Augustine said.

These views of Christ expressed by the evangelists are all influenced, to a greater or lesser extent, by the knowledge of the Risen Christ, the final chapter in the story. One of the attractions of Mark is that in many ways the Markan Jesus is the simplest and most human portrait. Already the Matthean portrait presents a more distant, stiffer and more hieratic Christ, who is addressed by his followers as 'Lord', and who is somehow seen by eyes aware that he is to be the Risen Lord. Finally in some ways the Johannine Christ seems hardly human at all, lost in the mysterious union of Father with Son – though in his tiredness and expression of emotion his subjection to the human condition is as clear in John as anywhere.

2 THE JESUS OF HISTORY

Since awareness broke upon the scholarly world that the evangelists are theologians in their own right and that they have played each an individual part in forming their material, there has been a renewal of what has been called 'the Quest for the historical Jesus'. In the understanding of the tradition, each layer of tradition has its own value. Just so, the historical basis of all the traditions has its own contribution to make to our understanding of Jesus. The expression comes from the English title of the book by Albert Schweitzer (1906), which summed up the first of the three phases.

The Quest for the historical Jesus

In 1778 H. S. Reimarus made the crucial distinction between the Jesus of history and the Christ of faith, indicating that the Christ of Christian faith is not necessarily in all respects the same as the historical Jesus. Perhaps the most important work of the Quest was the *Leben Jesu* (1835) of D. F. Strauss; he maintained that it is impossible to write a life of Jesus – though he himself was trying it – because the facts have been so embellished with myths by the gospel writers. The last work surveyed by Schweitzer was that of W. Wrede (1901); Wrede thought that Jesus had not himself claimed to be the Messiah, but had been claimed to be such only by the disciples. Schweitzer himself concluded that Jesus was a noble but mistaken apocalyptic visionary, who expected his death to usher in a new age. Thus it became clear in this first phase of the Quest that the understanding of Christ in the gospels could be different in various ways from Jesus' own self-understanding.

The New Quest

After the First World War research into the life of Jesus was eclipsed by the discoveries of form criticism. In 1926 R. Bultmann, the high priest of form criticism, declared in his book *Jesus* that we can know almost nothing about the historical Jesus. In critical circles this remained the prevailing view until Ernst Kaesemann's important article in 1953, 'The problem of the historical Jesus', which is generally held to have launched the New Quest. The first attempt in the post-Bultmannian era to write a life of Jesus was that of G. Bornkamm in 1956. Bornkamm's thesis was that one can still discern the unmatched authority of Jesus, 'The man who fits no formula', as he entitled the second chapter of his book *Jesus of Nazareth*.[1] This phase of the Quest concentrated on the sayings of Jesus rather than his actions, and was marked by attempts to formulate criteria for the authenticity of the words of Jesus (see pages 32–4).

The assured results were, however, meagre, and the disputes about authenticity continuous. A 'Jesus' seminar in North America found the position so uncertain that they even went as far as to try to establish the authenticity of sayings by majority vote![2]

Similarly, title-Christology seemed to have reached a dead end. In the era of O. Cullmann[3] and R. H. Fuller[4] the approach to Jesus had been through his titles. The way Jesus is presented in the New Testament was examined by means of an investigation of each of the titles given to Jesus, 'Son of God', 'Son of man', 'Messiah', and so on, a method which later became known as 'title-Christology'. Although it was accepted that these titles had been considerably developed in the early Christian communities, it was considered that there had been a foundation for each in Jesus' earthly life. Doubt was gradually cast, however, upon Jesus' use of one after another of the titles used in the gospel: it seemed highly unlikely that he had claimed the title 'Messiah' for himself; the expression 'Son of God' was found to have many shades of meaning and to require a good deal of unpacking rather than being a straightforward expression of divinity. The expression 'Son of man', on

---

[1] G. Bornkamm, *Jesus of Nazareth* (London, Hodder & Stoughton, 1960).

[2] P. Hollenbach, 'The historical Jesus question in North America today', *Biblical Theology Bulletin*, **19** (1989), pp. 11–22.

[3] O. Cullmann, *The Christology of the New Testament* (London, SCM, 1957).

[4] R. H. Fuller, *The Foundations of New Testament Christology* (Lutterworth, Lutterworth Press, 1965).

which so much had been built, was convincingly claimed by Geza Vermes[5] to be on Jesus' lips merely a circumlocution for the first-person pronoun, transformed into a title (with reference to Daniel 7:13–14) only by the evangelists.

The Third Quest

In the 1980s came a new thrust, though it is questionable whether this angle of research is sufficiently different to be called 'The Third Quest'. It consists in looking rather at the actions than the words of Jesus, as being a more secure basis of discerning the basic pattern of his life and ministry.

E. P. Sanders' view

The most persuasive approach is provided by Ed Sanders in a series of publications including *Jesus and Judaism* and *Jewish Law from Jesus to the Mishnah*.[6] Sanders finds the clue to Jesus' activity in his move against the Temple. It was this action which led swiftly to his execution. It was not, however, an isolated incident. As we have seen (pages 81–2), Jesus' threats against the Temple are among the best-attested of his sayings, and occur in several different forms. In what is now the opening of the eschatological discourse (Mk 13:1–4), Jesus predicts that no stone will be left upon another. At his trial this accusation is used, though Mark characterises it as a false charge. The memory of it recurs in the taunts by his opponents while he hangs on the Cross. Although Jesus' own action in the Temple can only have been symbolic – any more would have provoked immediate reaction from the Temple staff – his attitude would have been enough to provoke not only action by the authorities but also hostility from the populace, to whom the Temple was the sacred centre of their life.

If this incident is genuinely the clue to Jesus' thinking, it must link

---

[5] Geza Vermes, *Jesus the Jew* (London, Collins, 1973).
[6] E. P. Sanders, *Jesus and Judaism* (London, SCM, 1985) and *Jewish Law from Jesus to the Mishnah* (London, SCM, 1990).

positively with the whole of his mission. Sanders sees it as part of Jesus' thrust towards an eschatological renewal of Israel. The old order is to be superseded and Israel renewed. Not only in the later Old Testament but also strongly in the inter-Testamental writings, the rebuilding of the Temple is symbolic of the restoration of the community of Israel. According to Sanders, Jesus had no very clear idea – nor did he need to have – either what form this renewal was to take, or what part he himself was to play in it. He simply knew that the old order was to be destroyed and that God was present in his own ministry, bringing this about. Paul's earliest expectation is that the restoration will take place somehow in the skies (1 Th 4:17), and this is neither affirmed nor denied in the sayings of Jesus. In the absence of evidence to the contrary, it is not unreasonable to assume that Paul is merely carrying on Jesus' teaching. Indeed, Paul appeals to 'the Lord's own teaching' in this connection (1 Th 4:15). As to his own part, we know only that Jesus rode symbolically on an ass into Jerusalem, in a way which was rightly perceived by his followers as indicating that he was the humble king, or perhaps more exactly that his kingdom was for the poor and neglected.

Apart from this central thrust of Jesus' ministry, Sanders is sceptical about how much we can know about Jesus. He regards the majority of the controversy stories as the product of disagreement within the Christ-ian communities about legal observance, and of controversy between those who did not observe the Law and those – both within and outside the Church – who regarded it as binding. One of the major difficulties is that Mark at least makes Jesus far too sweeping in his abolition of the requirement to keep the Law; whether his followers must observe the Law was, after all, one of the principal areas of dissension within the early Christian communities (in the Acts of the Apostles, for example, and in the controversies at Antioch mentioned in Galatians 2:11–14). If Jesus had been so definite about the abolition of Jewish legal observances it is difficult to see that his followers could have gone back on the point and raised it all again. Sanders disputes not necessarily the genuineness of the controversy sayings themselves, but the context into which they are put by the gospel tradition; the sayings may be genuine, he argues, but the contents were evolved in order to settle problems of legal observance within Christianity.

There is a clash not only between Jesus' declaration that all food is clean and the subsequent tussle about this in the Church, but also between Jesus' attitude to the gentiles (the Syro-Phoenician, Mark 7:24–30) and the subsequent disagreements over the mission to the gentiles. How is it possible that Jesus confined his mission territorially almost exclusively to Galilee and Judaea, and that he referred to the

Syro-Phoenician woman as a *kunarion* (not to be translated hopefully and sweetly as 'housedog', but frankly and brutally as 'dog' – that was how Jews named gentiles), and yet that the gospels contain also such instructions as the finale of Matthew (undoubtedly Matthew's own composition), instructing the disciples to baptise all nations (Mt 28:19)?

Geza Vermes' position

Vermes' solution is that Jesus saw his mission as being to Israel. He was typical of the charismatic Galilean teachers such as Honi the Circle-Drawer: the stress of his teaching was typical of the teaching of these figures – he emphasised the Fatherhood of God, trust in God, and imitation of the holiness of God. It was only after his death that his followers transformed his legacy by introducing four principal changes:

1. they put aside his Jewish exclusiveness;
2. they abandoned the Law;
3. they transferred his present eschatological urgency to the future;
4. Paul's pessimism about human nature led him to see Jesus' death in the sacrificial terms of vicarious atonement for human sin.

In this case the Jesus presented in the gospels is a mere subsequent construct, a combination of two different angles of vision, one Jewish and one non-Jewish.

Conclusions

A more reliable approach is, however, to view the whole Jesus-tradition from one firmly established vantage point. Jesus' demonstration in the Temple may be taken as the basis: this was the climax and logical consequence of his offer of a renewal of Judaism. His controversies and teaching in Galilee all point towards such a renewal. When he came up to Jerusalem it was the inevitable consequence that he must announce the obsolescence of the Temple and its cult, since it was part of the Judaism which was to be superseded by the Judaism of the kingship of God.

With this as the starting point, it is possible to move to the detail.

1. *The Twelve* One of the most certain of Jesus' actions is the establishment of a group of twelve – their names vary from list to list, but their number is so firmly fixed that they are referred to as 'the Twelve' even when Judas' defection has reduced them to eleven. This must be seen in function of the Jewish hope for the restoration of the twelve tribes of Israel, frequently mentioned in Baruch, Ben Sira, 2 Maccabees and the inter-Testamental literature.

2. *The opening to the nations* It is an idea prominent in many of the later biblical books and the inter-Testamental writings, that at the restoration of Israel in the fullness of time, salvation would flow from Israel to all the nations. Thus the opening to the nations is the logical consequence of Jesus' own teaching, even if he did not himself take that step. Jesus cannot necessarily be expected to have had a plan of campaign fully worked out to the last detail, with consequences neatly prearranged and thought through.

3. *The Suffering Servant* This approach has the advantage of making sense also of the development of the attitude to Jesus' Passion. The well-attested sayings at the Last Supper provide sufficient evidence that Jesus was aware of that stream of Jewish thinking which sees persecution and martyrdom as the price of bearing God's message to those who will not accept it. The allusions in Jesus' sayings to the Song of the Suffering Servant are unmistakable indications of how he saw his mission. But they are no more than tactful allusions, more consonant with Jesus' speech than with invention by the early Church. He saw that his renewal of Judaism, his preaching of the kingdom, was to be a cause of opposition and rejection. Ever since the Suffering Servant poems of Deutero-Isaiah and especially since the Maccabean persecution, the idea of the death of God's Chosen One for the sake of others is so common in Judaism that the death of Jesus was almost bound to be viewed in this way. Again, Jesus may not have thought through the sacrificial aspect of his death in the same detail as Paul, but he must have been aware of it. Nor was it necessary that Jesus should foresee the details of his execution, or even the details of his vindication: his complete surrender to the Lord as the Suffering Servant is sufficient indication of his total offering and total confidence.

4. *The flight of the disciples* One further inescapable fact is the flight of the disciples at the Passion, and their total unpreparedness for the

Resurrection. Jesus' predictions of his future sufferings and vindication, and his promises of protection in times of persecution, cannot have been clear enough to prevent this cowardice.

The historicity of two sets of stories has not been touched in this discussion: the miracle stories and the personal stories about Jesus such as the Baptism and the Transfiguration.

There can be no doubt that Jesus worked miracles. Miracles as such are no sign of Jesus' uniqueness: he himself grants that other figures in the Jewish world worked exorcisms, when he was accused of casting out spirits by Beelzebul. Miracles of healing are claimed widely in the Hellenistic world (many of Jesus' miracles are paralleled in the inscriptions at Epidaurus, and in the activity of Apollonius of Tyana, as written up by Philostratus). In a pre-scientific age the concept of a miracle had no real place. The miracles of Jesus are more rightly regarded as wonders of God, evidences of the activity of God in Jesus, rather than strictly miraculous in the sense that certain miracles of Lourdes are claimed to be. Several of the accounts of the nature miracles are formed in such a way as to show the fulfilment of scripture (the Feeding of the Multitude, the Walking on the Water), and it is difficult to recover the factual events which underlie these accounts.

A second area which requires research is the so-called *Legenden*, such as the Baptism, the Temptations and the Transfiguration. Here the difficulty of recovering the events which underlie these stories, suffused as they are with biblical imagery, is compounded. Here again it is the quality of Jesus, seen and described with the help of the imagery, which is more important than any 'brute' facts which may underlie the account.

As we have seen constantly in the course of this study, Mark himself interpreted the material he received from the oral tradition by his combination of traditions, by his arrangements and his emphasis. He did this to underline the themes and aspects which seemed to him important, no doubt partly because of the circumstances of his community. He told the story in his own way and with his own style. We may surmise that this was the understanding and these were the skills which had brought the community to entrust this task to Mark, and then to accept his gospel as an accurate record of the Good News of Jesus.

3 PERSONAL STUDY

Write an essay: 'In what sense is the Gospel of Mark a true picture of Jesus?'

PART III

Luke: The gospel of the Spirit

CHAPTER 9

HOW DID LUKE SET ABOUT WRITING HIS GOSPEL?

1 LUKE'S TECHNIQUES IN WRITING

We may take it for granted that the Gospel of Luke and the Acts of the Apostles were written by the same author and so constitute one double volume, Luke–Acts. It will become clearer and clearer in the course of this study that the two documents form a pair, and indeed in the Preface to Acts the author mentions his 'earlier work' (Ac 1:1), which can be no other than Luke. The two works share a common approach, a common outlook, a common theology, and a distinctive common vocabulary.

The author was a skilled and versatile writer, capable of using widely differing materials and of composing in widely differing styles. If we may accept, at least as a working hypothesis, the conclusion of Chapter 2 that Luke is dependent on Mark and Matthew, it follows that he used those two gospels for the main body of his own gospel. Even here, however, he skilfully rearranged and pointed the material in order to express the emphases of his own or his community's message. In addition he composed with a considerably freer hand in the gospel at least the Infancy Narratives, some miracle stories and a number of parables; and the stories of the Resurrection Appearances, for which there is little or no parallel in Mark or even Matthew. For the Acts we do not have any of Luke's sources available to us, so we cannot tell to what extent or in what direction he has modified them. We may assume, however, that Luke acted in somewhat the same way as other writers of his time. His way of writing has been characterised as 'imitative historiography' – that is, the writing of history by means of imitation.

Luke and contemporary secular writing

Each half of Luke's double volume begins with an introduction, a feature which sets the work in a particular class of writing. Short treatises, of about the length of Luke's work, were common in those days, and it was a convention to begin with a preface similar to his, including such matters as the name of author and the recipient, the author's aim, the sources of his information, the importance of the subject, and a claim to personal competence for the task. Luke's preface accords with these conventions, though it has recently been shown[1] that in detail it is more similar to medical, mechanical, military and mathematical treatises than to historical works.

Verses 1:1–4 suggests that Luke builds on the experience of other evangelists, and that he writes 'in order'. This does not, of course, necessarily imply that the order is chronological, but only that it is ordered as Luke thinks it should be. So Luke's claim is not incompatible with the suggestion that in Acts Luke has formed three great missionary journeys of Paul out of far more disparate material, perhaps notes on several different smaller journeys.

It has long been recognised that Acts shows a convincing knowledge of material elements, such as magistrates and legal details. The constitutional details of different cities around the Mediterranean differed widely, their magistrates having different names and different powers, and all of these Acts gives correctly, mentioning, for example, the 'proconsul' as governing Cyprus, the 'generals' as magistrates at Philippi, and the 'Asiarchs' and the 'town clerk' as officials at Ephesus.

Not all details, however, may be assumed to be literally exact in the way expected of a modern historian. Since the time of Thucydides, five hundred years before Luke, it had been the convention that if a historian did not know what a speaker had said on a particular occasion, the historian would put in the speaker's mouth what would have been appropriate for him to say:[2]

> In this history I have made use of set speeches, some of which were delivered just before and others during the war. I have found it difficult to remember the precise words used in the speeches

[1] Loveday Alexander, *The Preface to Luke's Gospel* [Society for New Testament Study Monograph Series 78] (Cambridge, CUP, 1993).
[2] Thucydides, *The Peloponnesian War* (my translation), I:22.

which I heard myself, and my various informants have experienced
the same difficulty; so my method has been, while keeping as
closely as possible to the general sense of the words that were
actually used, to make the speakers say what, in my opinion, was
called for by each situation.

This became an important means whereby the historian could convey
his view of events. It became the convention for historians, before the
description of a battle, to put into the mouth of each opposing general
a speech to his troops, explaining the issues at stake, how things had
come to such a pass, and the likely consequences of defeat and victory.
(An excellent example is the speeches of the Roman and Scots generals
before the battle at the Mons Graupius – the Grampians? – which
finally secured England for the Romans. The Scottish general and the
Roman general each speak for two pages.[3]) These issues may well have
been in the mind of the generals, if they were sufficiently clear-sighted,
but it is hardly likely that generals would have spelled out these matters
to battle-hungry troops shivering in the Scottish drizzle; nevertheless,
it makes the historian's comment more dramatic and forceful than the
modern convention of frank admission that this is the historian's own
interpretation. Such a convention may well have been at work in the
reporting of speeches in Acts, particularly Stephen's speech before his
martyrdom.

Similarly, ancient historians were less meticulous about checking
individual facts. Quintilian, the contemporary arbiter of all style, allowed
the inclusion in a history of details typical of an event (such as the sack
of a town), even if these had not been recorded in the particular case.

Some of the scenes themselves also may be related to contemporary
literature.[4] There is a clear comparison between the story of the death
of Herod Agrippa in Acts and in Josephus (in the charmingly Victorian
translation of Whiston):[5]

A great multitude was gotten together of the principal persons
and such as were of dignity through his province. He put on a
garment made wholly of silver, and of a contexture truly wonderful, and came into the theatre early in the morning; at which time
the silver of his garment, being illuminated by the fresh reflection
of the sun's rays upon it, shone out after a surprising manner and
was so resplendent as to spread a horror over those that looked

[3] Tacitus, *Agricola*, Chapters 30–4.
[4] See Richard I. Pervo, *Profit with Delight* (Philadelphia, Fortress, 1987), for an extended
treatment.
[5] Josephus, *Antiquities of the Jews* (tr. William Whiston, London, Nelson, 1878), 19:8.

intently upon him; and presently his flatterers cried out, one from
one place and another from another, that he was a god . . . Upon
this the king did neither rebuke them nor reject their impious
flattery. But, as he presently afterwards looked up, he saw an owl
sitting on a certain rope over his head, and immediately understood
that this bird was the messenger of ill tidings, and fell into the
deepest sorrow. A severe pain arose in his belly and began in a
most violent manner. He therefore looked upon his friends and
said, 'I whom you call a god, am commanded presently to depart
this life' . . . And when he had been quite worn out by the pain
for five days, he departed this life.

The description of Josephus is fuller, showing that Agrippa deliberately
presented himself as the sun-god, and including the bird of ill-omen
and − too late! − a nice speech of repentance. Being struck by an
angel and eaten by worms (Ac 12:23) is simply a different piece of
folklore from the unexplained five-day pain of Josephus. They are
merely different ways of expressing divine punishment for claiming
divinity.

The similarities between Acts and other writings of the time, however, are not limited just to historical writing. Contemporary literature
included lighter entertainment, which also provided models for Luke.
The scene in Lycaonia (Ac 14:11–18) where Barnabas and Saul are in
danger of being offered sacrifice draws clearly and wittily on a popular
and well-known tale of Ovid.[6] The gods Jupiter and Mercury (in
Greek, Zeus and Hermes) wander through the Bithynian countryside,
unrecognised until the dear old long-married couple Baucis and Philemon entertain them devotedly. The old couple beg to be priests of
these gods and to die in the same hour. For their pains they are turned
into a double-trunked tree, locked in perpetual embrace. The crowds
in Lycaonia seem to be aspiring to the same divine favours, though
Ovid himself agreed that his story was pretty but incredible. In Acts
too the story is full of riotous improbabilities which cheerfully leave it
on the same level as a folk tale.

More generally, it must be admitted that the same motifs of
excitement − apart from sex − are used in Acts as in the contemporary
romantic, station-bookstall novels of Chariton, Achilles Statius, and (a
little later) Xenophon of Ephesus: suspense, intrigue, ambush, speedy
recovery after violent torture, rhetorical confrontations and law-court
scenes, crowds rapidly whipped up for the sake of drama, and shipwreck.

One of the most frequent motifs is unexpected release from prison.

[6] Ovid, *Metamorphoses* (my translation), 8:630–724.

An instance of this is the story of Peter's release from prison in Acts 12:1–19. It is full of wit, burlesque and reversal:

- not Peter but the guards are killed;
- Peter is let out of prison *by* an angel, and kept out of the house *as* an angel;
- it is doubtful whether Peter or Rhoda is the more dopey.

But of course to say this does not amount to denying that Peter was imprisoned by Agrippa and released in a way that the Christian community regarded as miraculous and heaven-sent. One might even hope that Luke appreciated Ovid's wit in describing Acoetes the Tyrrhenian's release from Pentheus' captivity:[7]

> Unbidden the doors spread wide,
> Unbidden, untouched by hand, the chains fell from his arms.

The same explanation may be used of Paul's release at Philippi (Ac 16:25–40), where folk motifs and improbabilities abound:

- the magistrates don't seem to notice that there has been a massive earthquake;
- the other prisoners stay meekly in the background;
- there is a nice little friendship novella about Paul breakfasting with the gaoler;
- the magistrates are brought to acknowledge God by Paul's slinky trick of declaring his Roman citizenship too late;
- and then why does Paul leave so suddenly after his triumph?

Luke and biblical writing

In the same way, and perhaps to a greater extent, Luke uses the Bible also for his allusive style of writing. The conversion of Saul (Ac 9:1–21) is recounted with the help of accounts of other biblical persecutors of God's people, Balaam (Nb 22–24) and Heliodorus (2 Mc 3:24–36):

- after the experience of God each of them needs to be led away, helpless, by his followers;
- each of them does the opposite of what he intended (Balaam blesses instead of cursing, Heliodorus offers sacrifice in the Temple he came to destroy);
- and each ends up by testifying to all about the work of the supreme God.

[7] Ovid, *Metamorphoses*, 3:699–700.

The purpose of this is to show the significance of the conversion of Paul: it is the conversion of a persecutor of God's people, turning him into an agent of God's glory. But the use of biblical imagery for a theophany does not invalidate the description of a religious experience which set the visionary on an opposite course.

The birth of the Church with the coming of the Spirit at Pentecost (Ac 2:1–13) is also full of biblical allusion. Understanding of these allusions is essential to the understanding of the significance of the scene:

1. A strong wind and fire are signs of the divine presence which occur also at the appearance of God to Elijah (1 K 19:11–12).
2. The principal allusion, which gives the sense of the whole scene, is to the extra-biblical Jewish tradition that at the giving of the Law on Sinai tongues of fire came upon the seventy elders (representing the conventional number of seventy nations of the world), as a symbol that the Law was to be given to all nations. In one sense this was considered to be the birth of the nation of Israel, as Pentecost is the birth of the new People of God. Here the nations of the world are represented in the list of nations who listened to Peter's speech.
3. Perhaps the overarching meaning is best given in Peter's explanation in his speech (Ac 2:14–21), that this moment is the fulfilment of the prophecy of Joel (3:1–5), 'I shall pour out my Spirit on all humanity . . .'.

In the gospel also, especially where Luke is not following Mark and so is composing more freely, biblical allusion is crucial to the understanding of Luke's meaning. This is particularly the case in the little episodes of the Infancy Narratives (Lk 1—2), the Opening Proclamation of Jesus in the synagogue at Nazareth (Lk 4:16–30), and such scenes as the raising of the Son of the Widow of Nain (Lk 7:11–17). These will be discussed in Chapter 12.

2 PERSONAL STUDY

1. How would you explain to a foreign friend the difference between reports in *The Times* and *The Daily Mirror*?
2. To what extent can you rely on Luke as a historian?

CHAPTER 10

LUKE'S PATTERNS OF THOUGHT

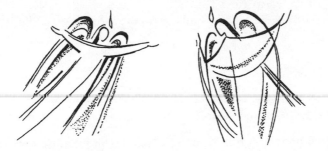

Every writer has characteristically personal patterns of thought by which he or she may be 'fingerprinted'. In the case of Mark certain (perhaps unconscious) techniques are easy to isolate (see pages 34–7). Luke also has patterns of thought which may be regarded as his own peculiar fingerprints.

1 THE FULFILMENT OF PROPHECY

To Luke prophecy is extremely important. It is connected with the twin themes of the presence of the Spirit which enables those who as so inspired to prophecy, and with the accomplishment of God's will. Luke frequently announces that such-and-such *must* happen ($\delta\epsilon\hat{\iota}$), with the understanding that this is in fulfilment of God's will. Thus 'I must be in my Father's house' (Lk 2:49); 'I must proclaim the good news' (4:43; also 9:22; 12:12; 13:14, 33, etc, though 'must' may be lost in translation).

Luke often gives a prophecy which, in the course of his work, he is careful to point out is fulfilled.

- The disciples are to shake the dust of unbelieving cities off their feet (Lk 9:5: fulfilled in Acts 13:51).
- Jesus' Passion prophecies (Lk 9:22, 44; 18:32–3 fulfilled in Lk 24:6–8, 44).
- His disciples will have the power to tread down serpents (Lk 10:19: fulfilled in Ac 28:3–6).
- His followers will have troubles (Lk 21:12–15: fulfilled in Ac 4:1–22; 5:17–42, etc.).

- They will be judges over Israel (Lk 22:30: fulfilled in Ac 5:1–11).
- They will receive power from on high (Lk 24:49: fulfilled in Ac 2:1–13).
- Baptism in the Spirit would follow 'not many days from now' (Ac 1:5: fulfilled in Ac 2:1–13).
- Agabus' prophecy of Paul's captivity (Ac 21:11: fulfilled in Ac 21:33).

2 PARALLELISM[1]

John the Baptist and Jesus

In the Infancy Narratives a careful parallel is pointed up between John the Baptist and Jesus:

	John	Jesus
The parents are introduced	1:5	1:26–7
The angel appears	1:11	1:26
The parent is troubled	1:12	1:29
'Fear not, a son will be born'	1:13	1:30–1
The mission and quality of the son	1:14–17	1:32–3
A question from a visionary	1:18	1:34
The reply from the angel	1:19–20	1:35–6
The final response from the parent	1:22 (signs)	1:38
The time comes for the birth	1:57	2:6
Rejoicing at the child	1:58	2:10
Circumcision and naming	1:59–62	2:21
A hymn	1:68–79	2:29–32
Wondering about the child's future	1:66	2:33
The child grows	1:80	2:52

This parallel is, as we shall see, not exact. It is tailored to highlight not only the similarities but also the contrast between the Baptist and Jesus. It is one of the means by which Luke shows the quality of John the Baptist, and the even greater quality of Jesus.

The gospel and the Acts

The most extended parallelism in Luke is between the gospel and the Acts. It is one of Luke's means of showing that the life and ministry of

---

[1] See Charles H. Talbert, *Literary Patterns, Theological Themes and the Genre of Luke–Acts* (Missoula, Scholars Press, 1971).

the Church continue the life and ministry of Jesus. Particularly this subserves the theme of the Spirit at work in the life of Jesus and of the early community.

	The gospel	Acts
Each begins with a prologue dedicated to Theophilus	1:1–4	1:1–2
The action starts with the descent of the Spirit (onto Jesus/the disciples)	3:21–2	2:1–4
– the Spirit descends in physical form	3:22	2:2–3
There is an opening proclamation in the power of the Spirit and on the fulfilment of prophecy	4:14–27	2:14–36
– which some reject	4:28–30	2:13
The authority of Jesus/Peter to cure is apparent	4:33–7	3:1–10
Numerous sick are brought to be cured	4:40–1	5:14–16
There are conflicts with religious leaders	5:29—6:11	4:1—8:3
Stephen's martyrdom mirrors that of Jesus:		
– the trial by religious leaders	22:66–71	6:8—7:57
– the refusal of the prisoner's witness	22:68	6:10
– 'the Son of man . . . at the right hand of God'	22:69	7:56
– this provokes the final reaction	22:71	7:57
– the execution outside the city	23:26	7:58
– the forgiveness of executioners	23:24	7:60
A centurion, respected by the Jews, sends messengers to fetch Jesus/Peter, asking for help	7:1–10	10:17–23
A widow and a raising of life come together	7:11–17	9:36–43
Paul's trial mirrors that of Jesus:		
– each is struck by the High Priest's men	22:63	23:2
– those in authority thrice declare him innocent	23:4, 14, 22	23:9; 25:25; 26:31
– a Herod hears the case	2:6–12	25:13–27
– the governor wishes to release him	23:16	26:32
– Jews shout, 'Away with him'	23:18	21:36

Peter and Paul

Besides repeating the story of Jesus, to some extent the story of the early community in the Acts forms a parallel history of the missionary activity of Peter and Paul. Luke is careful to show that their ministry is expressed in the same experiences and activities, many of which also occur in the ministry of Jesus. Luke's purpose here is to balance the two apostles, to show that they are the two great leaders of the nascent Church, who worked together, yet separately, to spread the faith. It also serves to suggest the unity of purpose in the apostolic Church, which is one of Luke's main concerns in the Acts.

	Peter	Paul
The manifestation of the Spirit	2:1–4	13:1–3
– leads to apostolic preaching	2:14–40	13:16–20
The healing of a lame man	3:1–10	14:8–10
– is followed by a speech	3:12–26	14:15–17
There is a confrontation with a magician	8:9–24	13:6–12
A dead person is raised to life	9:36–41	20:9–12
Peter/Paul is given divine reverence	10:25–6	14:13–15
Peter/Paul is miraculously liberated from prison	12:6–11	16:24–6

Similar patterns

Luke has other similar patterns on a smaller scale. He tends to think in patterns of pairs and fours. Thus, instead of Matthew's eight beatitudes, Luke has four beatitudes, balanced by four woes (Lk 6:20–6) and followed by four commands (6:27–30). There follow two more pairs of pairs (do not judge, do not condemn; forgive, give) in 6:37–8. Another four occurs in 14:12–13 (friends, brothers, relations, rich neighbours), and similarly in 21:16.

Perhaps more significant are instances where Luke cuts down to a pair what in Matthew was a triplet: for example, 'swept and tidied' in 11:25, omitting Matthew's 'unoccupied' (Mt 12:44); in 11:49 'prophets and apostles . . . slaughter and persecute' instead of Matthew's 'prophets and wise men and scribes . . . slaughter and crucify, . . . scourge' (Mt 23:34).

3 DRAMATIC SCENES

Luke has a genius for composing little dramatic scenes, many of them as the most important vehicles of his theological lessons. Some of these, the Opening Proclamation at Nazareth, Pentecost, and the Conversion of Paul, have already been mentioned. They are made more dramatic – and more suitable for performance – by the careful indication of entries and exits, and by dialogue between the characters. When Luke is composing with a free hand, but not therefore necessarily without traditional material (as may be seen in the case of the Opening Proclamation and the Ten Lepers), he delights in using this formula. Only a few among many such cases are here outlined.

1. The Opening Proclamation at Nazareth (Lk 4:16–30) begins with an entry ('He came to Nazara . . . and went into the synagogue'), continues with dialogue (built on the scene in Mark 6:1–6), and concludes with an exit ('he passed straight through the crowd and walked away').
2. The Cure of Ten Lepers (Lk 17:11–19) similarly begins with an entry ('ten men suffering from a virulent skin-disease came to meet him'), continues with dialogue (drawn from Mark's Cure of a Leper in Mark 1:40–5, but working in the very Lukan themes of a Samaritan, thanks, and giving glory to God), and ends with an implied exit ('go on your way').
3. The Interrogation of Herod (Lk 23:7–11) begins '[Pilate] passed him over to Herod', continues with an interrogation ('he questioned him at some length'), and ends 'he . . . sent him back to Pilate'.
4. On the Road to Emmaus (Lk 24:13–32) 'Jesus himself came up and walked by their side'; there follows the discussion on the fulfilment of scripture, until 'he had vanished from their sight'.
5. At the Ascension (Ac 1:6–12), 'having met together' they converse with Jesus till 'a cloud took him from their sight' and they 'went back to Jerusalem'.
6. For the Baptism of the Ethiopian (Ac 8:26–40), 'Philip ran up' and engaged the Ethiopian in dialogue on the fulfilment of scripture; and after the baptism Philip 'was taken away by the Spirit of the Lord', and the Ethiopian 'went on his way rejoicing' – rejoicing being another Lukan trait.

In the scenes of the Infancy Narratives the same technique is put to use[2] in both Annunciations, to Zechariah and to Mary, the Visitation,

[2] See R. Laurentin, *Structure et Théologie de Luc I–II* (Paris, Gabalda, 1957).

the Circumcision of the Baptist, the Nativity, the Presentation in the Temple and the Finding of Jesus in the Temple.

4 CHARACTERISATION

Luke stands out from the other synoptic gospels by his interest in human character. This emerges particularly, but not only, in the parables. In Mark's and Matthew's parables there are few characters, and those who do occur are simply human beings, or at most representatives of their profession or estate. Thus Mark has vinedressers, a master of the house, servants and a doorkeeper – all of whom remain faceless. Matthew has a king, a master of the house and a merchant: in all these cases it is transparently clear that the superior figure stands for God and the inferiors for human beings in general. In Matthew there is no representation of the varieties and complexities of human life, no interest in human situations, doubts, fears, self-questionings, moods, duplicity or dilemmas; virtually the only qualifications used are 'good' and 'bad'. Amounts of money are, after the manner of rabbinic parables, astronomical, in contrast on the one hand with Mark's peasant pittances and on the other with Luke's sensible commercial sums.

In Luke the characters spring from the page. To begin with, their situations are far more varied: an importunate midnight traveller and his unresponsive friend, a corrupt and shifty judge, a poor man covered with sores and befriended by dogs, a meticulous housewife, and a thoughtful Samaritan (who is generous, but cannily keeps the innkeeper on a short leash). The characters burst into direct speech, justifying themselves (Lk 11:7), complaining (13:7), mocking (14:30), sharing their joy (15:6), grovelling (15:21). The contrast between Matthew's and Luke's approaches may be illustrated from two parables.

1. *The Prodigal Son* (*15:11–32*) It is highly likely that this parable is Luke's own development of Matthew's Two Sons (21:28–32). Matthew has the typically Matthean stark opposition and contrast between the two sons, without a touch of humanity; there is no indication why they obey or disobey, or why the elder son changes his mind, or of the father's reaction. In Luke's hands this blossoms into the vibrant story of the younger son's breathtakingly brazen suggestion, his profligate way of life and repentance, contrasting with the unimaginative, industrious and resentful elder brother, while the tender-hearted and indulgent father strives at all costs to keep the peace between them.

2. *The Great Feast* (*14:15–24*) Matthew woodenly presents (22:1–10) a
king with groups of slaves, invited guests who simply go off about
their business, or even inexplicably kill the messengers, until the
king flies into unjustified rage and sends his armies to burn their
city. Everyone overreacts. By contrast Luke's host seems to have only
one overworked slave, who is sent rushing breathlessly about one
task after another. The invited guests think up grudging excuses,[3]
but do at least have the courtesy to make their apologies.

The contrast shows up not only in the parables, but also in the
Infancy Narratives. In Matthew there is no interchange between human
beings, no give-and-take, no warmth; Joseph does not even speak to
Mary about their problem. In Luke there are joyful parties at the birth
of children, warm family welcomes, and embraces – as well as the
bite of poverty. Mary even reproaches her truant son (Lk 2:48), then
wisely bites her lip at his typical twelve-year-old reply, 'Didn't you
know . . .'?

Another typical Lukan character is Zacchaeus (Lk 19:1–10), the black-
guard who makes good, vividly presented, as he rushes behind the backs
of the crowds to try to get a glimpse of Jesus, and bustles up and down
his sycamore tree. In the Acts (where no contrast between Luke and
the other gospels is possible), the same characterisation continues, with
Simon Magus' ingratiating little speech in his attempt to initiate simony
(Ac 8:19), Ananias' scared excuses to avoid facing Paul (9:13), the
affection everyone shows for kindly Dorcas (9:36–9), Peter's prissy
disgust when invited to eat unclean food (10:14), and the laughably
flustered Rhoda slamming the door in Peter's face (12:14).

What Luke gains in imagination, he sometimes lacks in logic, getting
things upside-down. There is no need to make signs to Zechariah (Lk
1:62); he is dumb, not deaf. The woman at Simon's house is forgiven
much because she loves much; Simon, by contrast, must learn that
people love much because they are forgiven much (7:40–50). The
parable of the Good Samaritan (10:29–37) is introduced to illustrate
whom I should help; in fact it illustrates the opposite, who helps me.

---

[3] In the gospel story itself Luke makes excuses for people when he can: the disciples
are startled out of sleep at the Transfiguration (Lk 9:32); they lie down, 'for sheer
grief' at the Agony in the Garden (22:45).

5 LANGUAGE AND IMAGERY

One of the most striking contrasts between Luke and the other evangel-ists lies in his use of a far more sophisticated language. The most notable cases are the prologues to his two volumes, which are composed in deliberate imitation of prologues to contemporary literary treatises. In each volume, both the gospel and the Acts, his vocabulary runs to over 2000 words, in contrast to Mark (1350 words) and John (1000 words). Most of his sophisticated style, such as his frequent use of the more elevated optative mood, is difficult to reproduce in English.[4] Goulder lists ten pages of special Lukan vocabulary, words and expressions which occur 'with markedly greater frequency in Luke than in Mark and Matthew'.[5] Many of these are quite complicated compound words, formed of a preposition joined to a verb. Luke also, for example, uses frequently the neat and sophisticated formula μέν ... δέ ... (= 'on the one hand ... on the other ..', e.g. Lk 3:16; 10:2), and such classical forms as ὀνόματι (= 'by name', e.g. 5:27; 23:50), or τοῦ with the infinitive to express purpose.

Luke's skill in language is shown by his ability to write in different styles. In the first two chapters of the gospel, and occasionally in other passages, he writes in conscious imitation of the Greek Bible (the Septuagint translation), in order to give the biblical atmosphere which is so important to the Infancy Narratives.

- A selection of such Old Testament phrases: 'in the sight of God' (Lk 1:6); 'as the custom was' (1:9); 'do not be afraid' (1:13); 'the time came for [name] to have her child' (1:57).
- Another Old Testament element is balancing phrases (the chief feature of Hebrew poetry):

'I am an old man
   and my wife is getting on in years'   (1:18);
'He will rule over the House of Jacob for ever
   and his reign will have no end'   (1:33).

These features contribute to Luke's emphasis that the message of the gospel is cradled in the Old Testament and the piety of the old Law.

This increased sophistication comes to view also in the imagery Luke uses. He moves in the bourgeois world of the city, far from Mark's

[4] See J. Fitzmyer, *The Gospel According to Luke, I–IX* [Anchor Bible Commentary, vol. 28] (New York, Doubleday, 1979), pp. 107–8.
[5] M. Goulder, *Luke – A New Paradigm*, vol 2 (Sheffield, Sheffield Academic Press, 1989), pp. 800–9.

primitive world of the countryside. Mark has fifty-one uses of imagery drawn from farm life, such as 'field', 'sow', 'seed', 'germinate', 'bear fruit', 'harvest'. Matthew doubles this number of countryside images, but then his gospel is twice as long, and contains many more than double the number of sayings, in which such imagery would occur. By contrast Luke, also double the length of Mark, has only fifty per cent more farm images; he is not interested in farm life. The mustard seed ends up not in a field but in a garden, and becomes not a shrub but a tree with branches, which is hardly accurate (Lk 13:19).

On the other hand, when it comes to economic life, Mark has only 8 images (9 uses): 'sell', 'barter', 'work', 'pay', 'make and lose money', 'measure', 'livelihood' – nothing sophisticated here! Matthew introduces 21 more images, making 29 in all. Luke drops some but introduces 27 new images, to reach a total of 48. This is where his interest and experience lie: 'creditor', 'debtor', 'do business', 'profit', 'lend', 'bill', 'steward', 'extort', 'exact', 'swindle', 'bank'. Goulder remarks[6] that he 'virtually leaves the countryside behind . . . Luke's own world is the town: debtors and builders and robbers and travellers, midnight visitors (friendly and otherwise), the wealthy and their guests'.

One difference is especially revealing for the worlds in which the three synoptics move – the money used. In Mark Jesus instructs the disciples to put no coppers in their purse (Mk 6:9): copper coins are all they are likely to have. He considers three hundred denarii (a year's wage for a casual labourer) to be a gigantic sum (Mk 14:5). Matthew allows the disciples no gold, silver or copper (Mt 10:9); this is the rabbinic world of dramatic exaggeration. In Luke they are to take no silver for the journey (Lk 9:3), a realistic prohibition for a comfortable world.

6 PERSONAL STUDY

1. What is the difference between the styles and the approaches of Mark and Luke?
2. Which do you prefer, and why?

---

[6] M. Goulder, 'Characteristics of the Parables in the Several Gospels', *New Testament Studies*, **19** (1968), p. 53.

LUKE AND THE SPIRIT IN ACTS

1 THE SPIRIT IN THE CHURCH ACCORDING TO PAUL

As a preliminary, it is important to recreate the context in which Luke wrote. We do not know exactly when or where he wrote. But the element which stands out in the churches of the East to which Paul wrote letters is the predominance of the Spirit and of Spirit activity. This is clear especially in Galatians, First Corinthians and Romans, and it may well provide a context for Luke's writings.

Galatians
As part of his complaint against the 'foolish Galatians' Paul appeals to the evidence of the Spirit among them:

> Having begun in the Spirit, can you be so stupid as to end in the flesh? Can all the favours you have received have had no effect at all — if there really has been no effect? Would you say, then, that he who so lavishly sends the Spirit to you and causes the miracles among you, is doing this through your practice of the Law . . .?
>
> (Ga 3:3–5)

The point here is that Paul can appeal to the visible manifestations of the Spirit as evidence that needs to be explained. Later in the letter also he appeals to the Spirit which enables us to cry 'Abba, Father' (4:6) and details the fruits of the Spirit as love, joy, peace, patience, and the rest (5:22). The Spirit was a very real presence in the community.

First Corinthians

The presence of the Spirit at Corinth needs no proof. The problem was rather that they were, so to say, hyperventilated. The Spirit was out of control, and Paul needs to detail ways in which their Spirit activity could be brought under control. He seeks to control it by placing the emphasis on the activities of the Spirit which build up the community. All the problems with which Paul deals in the last third of the letter are connected with their unbridled Spirit-filled way of life. Their liberty in the Spirit must be moderated by love. The gifts of the Spirit such as speaking in tongues are valuable only in so far as they serve the community.

Romans

In Romans, where the manifestations of the activity of the Spirit do not seem to have been so extreme, Paul can concentrate more on the vivifying role of the Spirit in Christians. It is in fact only in 1 Corinthians 15 that Paul uses the expression 'life-giving spirit' of the Spirit which is the Risen Christ, the Second Adam. But this is the background thought behind Romans 8, the chapter on the new creation in Christ, in which Paul mentions the Spirit no fewer than twenty-nine times (as opposed to five times in Romans 1—7). The whole creation is in the act of 'groaning in labour pains' – 'And not only that: we too, who have the first-fruits of the Spirit, even we are groaning inside ourselves, waiting in eagerness for our bodies to be set free' (8:22–3).

For Paul, then, the corporate and individual life of the Christian is intensely an expression and a manifestation of the Spirit. It provides an attractive and plausible background to suppose that a couple of decades later Luke looks back to the earliest days of the Church and sees the same.

THE SPIRIT IN THE CHURCH IN ACTS

a The birth of the Church

The coming of the Spirit gives birth and life to the Church. So after the Ascension the activity of the disciples is, so to speak, suspended until the coming of the Spirit: they are simply to go back to Jerusalem and wait till the Spirit comes (Ac 1:4). The scene of Pentecost is the first in Acts of Luke's great allusive theological scenes. We cannot be sure whether Pentecost was already celebrated at this time as the Feast of the Giving of the Law on Mount Sinai, but the scene is certainly full of reminiscences of the theophany on Mount Sinai. The significance of the event on Sinai is that it made Israel a nation, and at the same time a nation which was closer to God than any other nation, a special possession and a beloved child. Luke is explaining that at the moment of Pentecost the community of believers in Jesus acquired this identity, became the new Israel. Formed from Israelites, it was the fulfilment of the promises of Israel.

The new dimension, over and above the Sinai event, becomes clear both by the allusion to the tongues of fire (Ac 2:3 – in Jewish legend of the Sinai event fire fell in the desert on the seventy elders, representing the seventy nations of the world) and in Peter's speech immediately afterwards: the Spirit now extends to all nations. This is the import of Joel's prophecy, on which Peter's speech is a midrash: 'I shall pour out my Spirit on all humanity' (2:17).

b The ministers of the Church

After Pentecost the ministers and officials of the Church are always noted as being endowed with the Spirit. It is all the more remarkable that the Spirit does not come upon Matthias at his pre-Pentecost election (Ac 1:26) – he is the exception who proves the rule that the community of the Spirit is born at Pentecost. The Seven 'deacons', and particularly Stephen, are chosen because they are 'filled with the Spirit' (6:3, 5). As he comes to his final glimpse of the Son of man standing at God's right hand, we are again reminded that Stephen was 'filled with the Holy Spirit' (7:55). When Philip baptises the Ethiopian he is both led to him by the Spirit and later led away to continue his mission (8:29, 39).

The same is true of Paul from the very beginning of his apostolate. When he is cured of his blindness and sent on his mission by Ananias, he is sent in the power of the Spirit: 'Ananias . . . entered the house, and laid his hands on Saul and said, "Brother Saul, I have been sent by the Lord Jesus . . . so that you may recover your sight and be filled with the Holy Spirit" ' (9:17). Still more significant, the Holy Spirit is seen to be active in the appointment by the community of Barnabas and Saul as missioners. While they were worshipping and keeping a fast 'the Holy Spirit said' that these two were to be appointed (13:2). 'They [the prophets and teachers, or perhaps the community as a whole – the reference is unclear] laid their hands on them'. In the rabbinic tradition this imposition of hands amounted to a commissioning or transfer of authority. The two delegates go, then, as representatives of the community, which is also expressed as their being 'sent on their mission by the Holy Spirit' (13:4).

The elders, too, whom Paul establishes in his communities, are considered as drawing their authority from the Spirit, for Paul, in his turn, finally charges the elders of Ephesus in his farewell discourse to care for the flock 'of which the Holy Spirit has made you the guardians' (Ac 20:28).

Luke shows, then, an enduring and ubiquitous awareness that it is the Spirit who is active in the officers of the Church.

The 'Pentecost of the Gentiles'

The conversion of Cornelius and his household is, like the conversion of Paul, one of the events in the progress of the Church which is so significant that Luke relates it three times. The event itself is related in Acts 10:17–48. Peter tells the story to justify his conduct before the circumcised believers in Jerusalem (11:11–18), and again recalls it at the 'Council of Jerusalem' (15:7–9). The crucial element in this scene is not so much the baptism of the new converts, but the descent on them of the Spirit, in relation to which the baptism follows only as a confirmation, a sort of sacramental outward sign of their reception. This happening is often called the 'Pentecost of the Gentiles' because the same phenomena occur as occurred to the disciples at Pentecost: the Spirit comes upon them suddenly – and to the great astonishment of the Jewish believers, who did not reckon that the Holy Spirit would have any truck with gentiles – and results in the same speaking in tongues and proclamation of the greatness of God.

The significance of the event is that it is the first opening of the Church to gentiles. For Luke this is vitally important because the event of Jesus on the one hand is the expected fulfilment of the promises of Israel, but on the other hand is also wider, with the unexpected extension of those promises to the gentiles. This extension is initiated and led by the Spirit.

Incompleteness through lack of the Spirit

Luke wishes also to show the obverse of the coin, incompleteness through lack of the Spirit. This comes out chiefly in two places, Samaria and Ephesus. In each place baptism had occurred without the imparting of the Spirit, which is not without its problems. Luke Johnson remarks,

'Luke is not interested in constructing a self-consistent theory of sacraments'.[1]

At Samaria disciples had been baptised in or into ($\varepsilon\check{\iota}\varsigma$[2]) the name of Jesus (Ac 8:16). Perhaps Luke means to convey that they had been baptised into the company of Jesus, in the sense of putting themselves under the power of Jesus, entering his company and committing themselves to his cause, for this is frequently in Acts the meaning of the 'name' of Jesus. But there is something lacking to them, and it is only when Peter and John have laid hands on them that the Spirit comes on them. It is significant that the presence, or the effects of the presence, of the Spirit are visible (cf. page 124) and unworthily attractive to Simon the magician (Ac 8:18–19). Did it issue in the power to work miracles?

At Ephesus also there were disciples who had not received the Spirit, or indeed heard of the Spirit, having been baptised only with John's baptism of repentance. Their initiation was clearly incomplete. Being baptised in or into ($\varepsilon\check{\iota}\varsigma$) the name of Jesus by Paul, they received the Spirit and began to speak in tongues and to prophesy (19:1–6), a Lukan variation to the result of the reception of the Spirit at Pentecost.

Guidance of the Spirit

Another continuous feature of the Spirit in Acts is the guidance it gives in speaking and in making decisions.

1. As soon as the Spirit comes upon the apostles at Pentecost they are guided in what they say; they 'began to speak different languages as the Spirit gave them power to express themselves' (Ac 2:4). It is not easy to discern whether Luke is giving us to understand that they are 'speaking in tongues', glossolalia in the classic sense described and discussed by Paul in First Corinthians. This is suggested by the reaction of the hearers that they were proclaiming 'the marvels of God'. Luke Johnson likens the phenomenon to 'the ecstatic (speech-like) babbling that was widely associated with mantic prophecy'.[3] This would then accord with the laughter of some and the suggestion that they were drunk (2:13). On the other hand the fact that Luke uses the term 'in different languages' and that each bystander heard

---

[1] Luke Johnson, *The Acts of the Apostles* [*Sacra Pagina* series] (Collegeville, Liturgical Press, 1992) p. 57.

[2] In popular Greek of the time the preposition is often used interchangeably, so that the shade of meaning is unclear.

[3] Johnson, p. 42.

in his own language indicates that real languages were being spoken, and that they were proclaiming an intelligible message. Possibly, of course, Luke had failed to think through the distinction, and is describing both phenomena at once.

2. There can be no doubt that Peter is guided to proclaim an intelligible message when, 'filled with the Spirit', he begins to preach before the Sanhedrin (Ac 4:8). Similarly Stephen and the others are filled with the Spirit as Stephen begins his speech. There, of course, he is fulfilling the prophecy of the gospel (compare Acts 6:10 with Luke 21:14–15): 'Make up your minds not to prepare your defence, for I myself shall give you an eloquence and a wisdom that none of your opponents will be able to resist or contradict'. Later, Apollos preaches 'with great spiritual fervour' – literally, 'boiling with the Spirit' (Ac 18:25).

3. At every step the movements of the Church and its missioners are guided by the Spirit. The letter conveying the decision of the 'Council of Jerusalem' records that 'It has been decided by the Holy Spirit and by ourselves' to impose certain regulations on gentile Christians to live together in harmony (Ac 15:28). The route of Paul and Timothy is determined by the Spirit, which tells them not to preach in Asia (16:6) or Bithynia (16:7). Then again the vision of the Macedonian beckoning them to Macedonia is clearly an indication from the Spirit (16:9). In the Western Text[4] the Spirit again sends Paul back to Asia (19:1). Paul's final important mission to Jerusalem, which results in his captivity and journey to Rome – the climax and conclusion of Acts – is no less prescribed by the Spirit, for he goes to Jerusalem 'in captivity to the Spirit' (20:22), and it is repeatedly stressed that this journey is directed by the Spirit (20:23; 21:11). Luke is not one for letting go by default a point he wants to make.

It is clear, then, that for Luke the Spirit is the life and inspiration of the nascent community, prescribing, teaching, and guiding.

---

[4] A certain group of manuscripts of the text of the Acts, of which the most important is the Cambridge manuscript 'Codex Bezae', represents a coherent tradition different from and slightly longer than the manuscripts stemming from the eastern Mediterranean. The text is known as 'the Western Text'. Scholars are undecided about which text is original. See W. A. Strange, *The Problem of the Text of Acts* [Society for New Testament Studies Monograph 71], Cambridge University Press, 1992.

3 PERSONAL STUDY

1. Is the presence of the Spirit in the Church noticeable today, and how?
2. Was it any different in Luke's day?

CHAPTER 12

LUKE AND THE SPIRIT IN JESUS

In his presentation of the work of the Spirit in Acts, Luke takes as his starting point the experiences of the Christian community in the first generations of the Church, when the activity of the Spirit was visible and palpable, unmistakable evidence which (as Paul shows) could be referred to and which demanded an explanation. But the Holy Spirit at work in the Church was the Spirit of Jesus, and the same activity of the Spirit was of course visible in Jesus' own life. Thus Luke's Christology – the aspects of Jesus which he particularly emphasises – centres on the Spirit manifested in the life of Jesus. His thought works, so to speak, backwards: from the experience of the Spirit in the community, through the Spirit in the first days of the Church, back to the Spirit in the life of Jesus. This is, as we have seen (page 117) not the only respect in which the gospel and the Acts form a diptych, each panel responding to the other.

1 THE SPIRIT IN THE INFANCY STORIES

In the Infancy Stories Luke works with more liberty than in the body of the gospel, where he is following the Markan tradition more closely. Here the action of the Spirit is particularly clear, at work in parallel in preparing John the Baptist and Jesus:

1. At the two Annunciations, to Zechariah and to Mary: 'from his mother's womb he [John] will be filled with the Holy Spirit' (Lk 1:15); 'The Holy Spirit will come upon you [Mary]' (1:35).
2. At the Visitation, Elizabeth is 'filled with the Holy Spirit' (1:41), and Mary's spirit 'rejoices in God my Saviour' (1:47).

3. At the circumcision of John, Zechariah similarly is 'filled with the Holy Spirit' (1:67) and is led to pronounce his canticle of the Benedictus. At the presentation of Jesus in the Temple, Simeon has received a revelation from the Spirit and is led into the Temple by the Spirit (2:26–7) to pronounce his canticle of the Nunc Dimittis.

2 THE SPIRIT AT THE BAPTISM OF JESUS

In the Gospel of Mark Jesus 'was baptised in the Jordan by John. And at once, as he was coming up out of the water, he saw the heavens torn apart and the Spirit, like a dove, descending on him' (Mk 1:9–10). Luke's version is subtly different in several respects:

1. John the Baptist plays no part in the scene; his arrest has just been narrated, which carries the suggestion that he is away from the scene, in prison. Some have interpreted this as an expression of a clear division in Luke between the two eras respectively of John the Baptist and of Jesus. In any case, Luke does not want to distract attention at this moment from the central figure.

2. The scene is no longer, as in Mark, the baptism of Jesus *and* the descent of the Spirit, but would be more aptly named the descent of the Spirit *on the occasion of* Jesus' baptism. The actual baptism is recounted only in a subordinate clause, as a sort of time-marker: 'it happened that . . . while Jesus after his own baptism was at prayer . . . the Holy Spirit descended' (Lk 3:21–2). In Luke, therefore, the scene should more properly be entitled not 'the Baptism' but 'the Descent of the Spirit after the baptism'.

3. The mention of Jesus being at prayer increases its importance, for Luke shows Jesus at prayer at several turning points – not only where Mark does, in the desert (Mk 1:35, cf. Lk 5:16) and at the Agony (Mk 14:32–40, cf. Lk 22:40–6), but also on the special occasions of the Choice of the Twelve (6:12), at Peter's crucial Profession of Faith (9:18–21), the Transfiguration (9:28–9), and when he teaches the disciples to pray (11:1–4).

4. Luke's slight change of expression from 'the heavens torn apart' (Mk 1:10) to 'heaven opened' (Lk 3:21) changes this from an allusion to Isaiah 63:19 to an allusion to Ezekiel 1:1, the awesome Vision of God enthroned on the Chariot-throne, which bulked so large in Jewish thought and mysticism; it therefore slightly increases the awe of the scene.

The significance of the scene is also apparent from its parallel in the

Acts: the descent of the Spirit on the apostles at Pentecost marks the beginning of the life and mission of the Church. Just so, the descent of the Spirit on Jesus at his baptism marks the beginning of his mission and apostolate. The changes which Luke effects in the baptism scene give the clue to how he sees the mission of Jesus which follows from it.

3 THE OPENING PROPHETIC PROCLAMATION

Just as the descent of the Spirit at Pentecost is immediately followed by Peter's proclamation that the era of the Spirit has begun, so the descent of the Spirit on Jesus is followed by his Opening Proclamation in the synagogue at Nazareth (Lk 4:16–30). Luke has taken from Mark the scene of Jesus' rejection at Nazareth and filled it out with his Opening Proclamation in the strength of the Spirit. In accordance with the parallel in Acts between Peter and Paul, this scene too is clearly reminiscent also of Paul's proclamation at Antioch (Ac 13:14ff.): both enter the synagogue on the Sabbath and are invited to speak and comment on the scripture.

The whole scene is the proclamation of a prophet.

1. Jesus came into Galilee like a prophet in the power of the Spirit (Lk 4:14). The early part of the proclamation (16b-20) is carefully constructed on a chiasmus (see page 35), balancing inwards to show that the centre and purpose is the prophetic theme of the forgiveness of sins:

    a he stood up
       b he was given the scroll and unrolled it
          c to proclaim
             d liberty
             d' liberty
          c' to proclaim
       b' he rolled up the scroll and gave it back
    a' he sat down.

2. The prominent saying of verse 24 presents Jesus as a prophet not accepted in his own country, confirmed at the end of the speech in the attempt to eliminate Jesus by throwing him off the cliff (4:29).

3. The latter half of the speech compares Jesus' ministry to that of the prophets Elijah and Elisha, suggesting that his ministry too is prophetic.

4 OTHER OCCASIONS WHEN JESUS IS SEEN
AS A PROPHET

On other occasions also Jesus' ministry is seen as prophetic, both in his actions and in the stress on fulfilment of prophecy.

The Son of the Widow at Nain

At the raising of the Son of the Widow of Nain (Lk 7:11–17) Jesus is acting as Elijah. The whole story is very similar to the story of Elijah's raising of the widow's son to life, but especially the verse he 'gave him to his mother' (Lk 7:15, cf. 1 K 17:23). It is remarkable also that the setting is precisely the district of Galilee where Elijah's ministry was centred. The reaction of the onlookers confirms the impression, for it is as a prophet that they hail Jesus, 'A great prophet has risen up among us' (7:16).

Comparison with John the Baptist

Luke also quotes the popular opinion that Jesus is a prophet like John the Baptist or one of the ancient prophets. But whereas Mark allows Herod to express the view that Jesus is a John returned to life, in Luke Herod is not allowed to stop there: 'John? I beheaded him. So who is this I hear such reports about?' (Lk 9:9).

The journey to Jerusalem

The whole great journey to Jerusalem which dominates the latter part of the gospel is put under the sign of the journey of a prophet going up to Jerusalem to be killed, for Jesus protests 'it would not be right for a prophet to die outside Jerusalem' (Lk 13:33), and his lament over Jerusalem – a city which Luke values so much – begins, 'Jerusalem, Jerusalem, you that kill the prophets and stone those who are sent to you' (13:34). Correspondingly, at the very end of the journey, as he approaches Jerusalem, Jesus prophetically weeps over the city's refusal to accept him, 'If you too had only recognised on this day the way to peace' (19:42).

The Road to Emmaus

On the road to Emmaus the disciple even sums up Jesus' whole ministry as that of a prophet 'who showed himself a prophet powerful in action and speech before God and the whole people' (Lk 24:19). In his explanation of the events which have taken place in Jerusalem, the Risen Christ starts with Moses and goes through all the prophets (24:27). From the similarity between the language used in his account of the

Road to Emmaus and that used in Acts 3:21–3, we may legitimately deduce that Luke as he wrote his gospel was recalling this passage in Acts, in which 'Moses' referred to Jesus, when

> God proclaimed, speaking through his holy prophets. Moses, for example, said, '*From among your brothers God will raise up for you a prophet like me . . .* '

This also serves Luke in conveying the sense of the presence of Moses with Elijah at the Transfiguration: the two represent the prophets, now supporting Jesus as the final prophet who fulfils this prediction.

Furthermore, Luke Johnson suggests that Stephen's interpretation of Moses in his speech gives the clue to the whole schema of Luke–Acts.[1] Moses was first rejected by his brothers: 'He thought his brothers would realise that through him God would liberate them, but they did not' (Ac 7:25) and rejected his leadership. But after he had gone away, he returned to be 'both leader and redeemer' (Ac 7:35). In the same way, Jesus was first rejected by Israel, and then – through his Spirit in the community – won acceptance among the true members of Israel. The first moment is represented by the gospel, the second by the Acts.

5 PROPHECY FULFILLED IN LUKE AND ACTS

The presence of the Spirit in the events of the gospel and the birth of the Church can be felt also in the fulfilment of prophecy in these events, on two levels. As the Spirit of God guided the prophecies of scripture, so it guides and achieves their fulfilment; as it guides the words and actions of the characters, so it guides and achieves the fulfilment of their predictions.

The Infancy Stories
In the Infancy Stories, the stress in the Old Testament piety of all the recipients and their eagerness to fulfil the requirements of the Law is directed to showing that the story is in sequence with the promises of the Old Law. The prophecies of Nathan to David are fulfilled at the Annunciation to Mary, and her Magnificat is full of the themes of the prophets, such as raising the poor and lowly, which come to their fulfilment in those events. Thus these are represented as the longed-for fulfilment of all the prophecies.

---

[1] Luke Johnson, *The Acts of the Apostles* [*Sacra Pagina* series] (Collegeville, Liturgical Press, 1992), pp. 120–2.

The fulfilment of earlier prophecies

Throughout the sequence of Jesus' life Luke is careful to stress that Jesus' actions are in accordance with the determined will of God. This is the meaning of the repeated δεῖ (= 'it is necessary'), which occurs twelve times of Jesus' actions and sufferings, examples being Luke 2:49, 'I must be in my Father's house', and 24:7, 'the Son of man was destined to be handed over into the power of sinful men'. Another frequent expression of the determinant will of God is expressed by the verb μέλλει (= 'it is destined'), as in 9:31, 'his passing which he was destined to accomplish in Jerusalem', and 24:21, 'Our own hope had been that he was the one destined to set Israel free'. By this means Luke shows that the course of Jesus' ministry was fixed beforehand by the prophesied will of God.

The fulfilment of gospel prophecies

Frequently in the course of the gospel, prophecies are made which are later seen being fulfilled. The primary case is that of the three great predictions of the Passion, which occur also in the other synoptic gospels. Luke also shows the fulfilment of the instructions of the disciples, that they are to shake the dust of unbelieving cities off their feet (Luke 9:5; 10:11, fulfilled in Acts 13:51); that they are to be persecuted and brought before governors and kings (Luke 21:12–15, fulfilled in the persecutions and imprisonment of the apostles, and the appearance of Paul before Felix, Festus and Agrippa, Acts 4:1–31; 6:10; 12:1–5; 24:1—26:32); that they are to be judges over Israel (Luke 22:30, fulfilled in Peter's judgement of Ananias and Sapphira, Acts 5:1–11); and that they are to be clothed with power from on high (Luke 24:49, fulfilled throughout the Acts). Within the Acts, too, Paul knows that he is destined to imprisonment and persecution at Jerusalem (20:22–3), which is soon afterwards foretold also by the prophet Agabus (21:10–11).

In these ways an air of destiny fulfilled according to the will of God hangs over the whole double volume. All of these crucial events are not only guided by the Spirit but foreseen in the revealed will of God. Nothing happens by chance or coincidence, but only according to what has been decreed beforehand. Jesus, himself the prophet, is only acting within the greater prophetic framework of Israel's destiny. This is all part of Luke's conception that the whole of salvation history is under the control of the Spirit of God, who is guiding and arranging events in every detail.

6 PERSONAL STUDY

1. What do you look for in a prophet today?
2. In what sense was Jesus this sort of prophet?

CHAPTER 13

WHO IS TO BE SAVED?

The four evangelists have special concerns and special points of view, which are no doubt to some extent the product of their environments, as they either build upon or react to these, and partly the result of their own temperaments and interests. For each of them the Good News of Jesus comes into a special context, so each considers that message against a different backcloth. Luke emphasises that the Good News of Jesus has come primarily to outcasts and rejects, those outside Israel (the promised recipient of salvation), women, the poor, and above all sinners.

1 LUKE AND THE DESTINY OF ISRAEL

The message of Jesus was that the fulfilment of the promises made to Israel had come, and yet this message was not accepted by the majority of God's People of Israel. This left Christians with a puzzle about the relationship of Israel to the Good News. Luke's presentation represents the masses of the people as sympathetic to Jesus, but the leaders obstinately refusing to accept him, so that his apostles were forced to turn to the gentiles. In fact, by the end of the first century a division between Christianity and Judaism had become firm and even hostile. The fact that Judaism failed to accept the message of Jesus has often been linked historically to the Sack of Jerusalem, as a visible sign of the bankruptcy of Israel.

The dating of the gospels

A factor which must have influenced Christian thinking was the Sack of Jerusalem. Jerusalem and its Temple were sacked by the Romans in AD 70, after a four-year rebellion. But it is quite unclear at what date the gospels were written, whether before or after this date. Conventionally Mark, the first gospel, is dated 65–75, but without very good grounds. Matthew shows signs of a deepening split between Christians and Judaism: he speaks of 'their synagogues' (4:23; 9:35; 10:17; 12:9; 13:54), implying a distinction from 'our synagogues'. There is an ongoing dispute whether the fuller details in the prophecy of the Sack of Jerusalem in Matthew 24 are shaped after the event from what actually happened, or are simply conventional prophetic language, indicating that the destruction fulfils the prophecies. If the latter, then obviously the fuller details are no indication that the passage was written after the event.[1]

The other clue to the dating of Matthew used to be considered the 'Curse of the Heretics'. The Jewish prayer called 'The Eighteen Benedictions (or Blessings)', which is said three times a day, contains one prayer which is in fact a curse on heretics, praying for their destruction. The Talmud says that this curse was composed towards the end of the first century, which would seem to indicate that the split between Church and Synagogue was complete by then. This would chime in with passages in John (9:22; 12:42; 16:2) in which the Jews threaten to exclude followers of Christ from the synagogue, and would suggest that John's gospel was written at about the same time. However, recent research[2] has established that the curse was directed against divergent Jewish groups in general rather than Christian Jews in particular. Although Justin Martyr in the second century says that the Jews slander and mock Jesus after their prayers (*Dialogue*, 137:3), St John Chrysostom two hundred years later still needs to persuade Christians not to attend Jewish synagogues. So even then the break was not complete.

This external evidence, of hostility between Christians and Jews, cannot then be used to date either Matthew or Luke with any accuracy. The evidence of the Acts about Saul's persecution of Christians before his conversion, and about the attempts of the Jewish authorities to eliminate him after his conversion, shows more than a mere personal enmity, but the evidence does not permit us to place this text in the atmosphere of any one decade of the late first century rather than any other.

[1] See Graham N. Stanton, 'The Gospel of Matthew and Judaism', in *Bulletin of the John Rylands Library* 66 (1984), pp. 264–84, now in his book *A Gospel for a New People* (Edinburgh, T. & T. Clark, 1992).

[2] Summarized by Pieter W. van der Horst, 'The *Birkat haminim* in recent research', *Expository Times* 105 (1994), pp. 363–8.

Salvation promised to Israel, but only partially accepted

From the beginning, Luke stresses that Jesus brings salvation to Israel.
It is important that he should do so, for the prophecies were made to
Israel. Even though not all Israel accepts the salvation[3] offered to them,
at least some part of the People of God do so.

1. The strongly biblical atmosphere of the first two chapters, and the
   constant stress that all the participants are faithful to the Law, indicate
   that Jesus comes to the faithful of Israel: 'according to the promise
   he made to our ancestors – of his mercy to Abraham and to his
   descendants for ever' (Lk 1:55). They are the spearhead of the faithful
   People of God, and especially of those particularly favoured by God
   in the prophets and the later tradition of Israel, the Poor of Yahweh.
2. Even when Luke is concentrating on the acceptance of Jesus by the
   gentiles, in the person of the centurion of Capernaum, Jesus is still
   seen to be aware of the claims of Israel. By a slight change, from
   οὐδενί to οὐδέ, where Matthew has 'in no one in Israel have I
   found faith as clear as this' (Mt 8:10), Luke has altered this to 'not
   even in Israel' (Lk 7:9), implying that in Israel at least some faith has
   been found.
3. On the way to Calvary and after the Crucifixion itself Luke stresses
   that the masses were brought to repentance: 'Large numbers of
   people' – and Luke uses the term normally used for the People
   of Israel as a sacred nation – 'followed him . . . and lamented for
   him' (Lk 23:27). After the Crucifixion, 'all the crowds who had
   gathered for the spectacle . . . went home beating their breasts'
   (23:48), showing that Jesus had the sympathy and understanding of
   the masses. Luke deliberately distances the masses from the leaders
   who were responsible for the condemnation of Jesus.

   In the Acts the same emphasis continues. The promises were made

---

[3] 'Salvation' is itself a Lukan concept. The verb 'to save' occurs, of course, in the other
gospels, but 'salvation' only in John (4:22, 42) and in Luke (five times in the gospel,
nine times in Acts). 'Saviour' occurs twice in Luke, twice in Acts and once in John
(4:42). In the Old Testament, and especially frequently in Deutero-Isaiah, God is the
Saviour of Israel. This thought is so frequent that salvation is conceived as something
awaiting Israel. To other nations it comes only through Israel. In Luke also the Saviour
is primarily God, who has sent his salvation to his people, but – and this is in itself
an important sign of Luke's Christology – the title is also transferred to Jesus: 'a
Saviour is born to you this day' (Lk 2:11) and 'God had now raised him up to be
leader and Saviour' (Ac 5:31), or 'Only in him is there salvation, for of all the names
in the world given to men, this is the only one by which we can be saved' (Ac
4:11–12).

to Abraham and his descendants. Peter underlines this to the crowds after the Healing of the Lame Man in the Portico of Solomon (Ac 3:13). Paul stresses that God raised up Jesus to fulfil his promises to David (13:23). In fact Luke notes that at any rate large numbers of the Jews were converted: three thousand on the day of Pentecost (Ac 2:41), soon rising to five thousand (4:4). The numbers of disciples at Jerusalem continued to increase (6:1). Although it is true that on the whole the opposition to Paul's preaching as he journeys round the Jewish cities of the eastern Mediterranean comes from the Jews, Luke often notes that some of them became believers — at Iconium a great many Jews and Greeks became believers (14:1), at Beroea 'many of them became believers' (17:12), and at Rome 'some were convinced' (28:24).

But the interpretation of history which Stephen gives in his great speech depicts Israel as constantly rejecting the message of the prophets. Moses was rejected by his people when he tried to bring peace to them, and had to flee away. When he returned, they again refused to listen to him. Stephen depicts Moses as a type of the final prophet, Jesus, and reproaches his hearers, the members of the Sanhedrin, 'You stubborn people . . . you are always resisting the Holy Spirit, just as your ancestors used to do . . . They killed those who foretold the coming of the Upright One, and now you have become his betrayers' (Ac 7:51–2).

Israel's salvation passes to the gentiles

One of the most marked features of Paul's missionary work in Acts is that on three solemn occasions, in the three main areas of his apostolate, he is forced to turn from the Jews to the gentiles, which he does each time with a formal biblical gesture. He makes a practice always of preaching first in the synagogues, but three times Luke notes that the hostility of the Jews forces him out. This occurs first in Asia, at Antioch in Pisidia; here, as the leading men of the city expelled Paul and Barnabas from their territory, 'they shook the dust from their feet in protest against them' (13:51). Next in Greece, at Corinth, 'he took his cloak and shook it out in front of them', with the symbolic words, 'Your blood be on your heads; from now on I will go to the gentiles with a clear conscience' (18:6). Finally at Rome, in the face of Jewish scepticism, Paul quotes to them Isaiah 6:9–10 and affirms 'You must realise, then, that his salvation has been sent to the gentiles' (28:28).

The theme of salvation being brought to the gentiles is, of course, of major importance in the whole construction of the Acts. It is because Paul is the apostle to the gentiles that his conversion is important enough to be recounted three times (in Acts 9, 22 and 26). Similarly the acceptance of the first gentile into the Christian community is recounted three times, once when it occurs (Ac 10), once when Peter justifies his conduct to the community at Jerusalem (11:1–17), and again by allusion (15:7–9). The divine will behind this event is further stressed by the facts that it is sponsored by Peter, the chief of the apostles, and that the Holy Spirit anticipates Peter's action by coming upon them – just as the Spirit came upon the apostles at Pentecost – spontaneously, even before Peter can baptise them (10:44–8). It is further stressed by a device which Luke uses frequently to underline the divine will, a double vision: Peter is told by the Spirit of the men who have come to fetch him and take him to Cornelius' house (10:19), and Cornelius 'was told by God through a holy angel' to send the men (10:22).

But already, in the gospel, the reader has been constantly reminded that the salvation brought by Jesus is for the gentiles:

1. In the Temple Simeon promises that Jesus will be 'a light of revelation to the gentiles' as well as 'glory for your people Israel', and indeed the gentiles are here mentioned before Israel (Lk 2:29–32).

2. In his first programmatic proclamation in the synagogue at Nazareth Jesus makes clear that his mission, as that of Elijah and Elisha in part, is to the gentiles, even to the exclusion of the Jews (4:24–7). This is fulfilled in the healing of the gentile centurion's boy, in which Luke warmly stresses the merits of the gentile, who has built the synagogue for the residents of Capernaum (7:1–10).

3. The Samaritans are especially favoured by Luke, perhaps because, as the nearest neighbours of the Jews, they were the most especially hated gentiles. So Luke tells the parable of the Good Samaritan (10:29–37). He also constructs from Mark's story of the Cure of a Leper (Mk 1:40–5; cf. Lk 5:12–16) another story, the Cure of the Ten Lepers, only one of whom returns, praising God, to thank Jesus (both typically Lukan elements of the story) – and this one is a Samaritan (17:11–19).

4. In the parable of the Great Feast (Lk 14:16–24), while Matthew concentrates on the punishment of those who refuse the invitations (Mt 2:2–10), Luke makes a little allegory to show the importance of an invitation to the gentiles; the messengers first bring in the crippled and beggars from the city (often representing the Chosen People), and then go out a second time beyond the city into the highways and byways, so beyond the Chosen People to the gentiles (14:21–3).

5. In the final charge to the apostles, the Risen Lord instructs them to preach repentance not merely to Israel but to all nations, beginning

from Jerusalem (24:46–7). This is, of course, exactly the programme of Acts. This was perhaps already hinted when the Lord sent out seventy-two disciples ahead of him to preach (10:1), for this is the traditional number of the nations of the world, indicating one disciple per nation.

2 LUKE AND WOMEN'S RIGHTS

Just as Luke is careful to show that salvation is not confined to Israel, so he is careful to show that it is not confined to males. In the other gospels one has the impression that the followers of Jesus are at least principally male. Luke seemingly deliberately pairs women with men, showing that salvation comes to both sexes. Thus:

- Zechariah and Mary receive the message of the births, to the credit of the female and the discredit of the male (Lk 1:11–20; 26–38);
- Simeon and Anna welcome Jesus in the Temple (2:22–38);
- the Widow of Zarephath and Naaman are mentioned as recipients of the prophetic miracles which are models of those of Jesus (4:26–7);
- a boy (the son of the Widow of Nain) and a girl (the daughter of Jairus) are raised from death to life (7:11–15; 8:41–56);
- the Queen of the South and the men of Nineveh will rise up to condemn the present generation (11:31–2);
- two miracle stories open 'and there before him was a woman' (13:11) and 'Now there before him was a man' (14:2);
- one parable presents a man, the Friend at Midnight (11:5–10), as a model of prayer; another presents a woman, badgering the Unjust Judge (18:1–8), as a similar model of perseverance in prayer;
- one parable shows a man searching for the Lost Sheep (15:4–7), the next a woman searching for the Lost Coin (15:8–10).

In the Acts:

- blame falls on both Ananias and his wife Sapphira (5:1–11);
- Aeneas and Tabitha, a man and a woman, are both healed, at the neighbouring towns of Lydda and Jaffa (9:32–42 [Lydda, or Lod, is now the airport for Tel Aviv-Jaffa]);
- Dionysius and Damaris, a man and a woman, become believers at Athens (17:34).

Luke is the only evangelist to mention the women who follow and minister to Jesus (8:1–3), and the women of Jerusalem who mourn for Jesus on the way to Calvary (23:27). Mary is also mentioned as present among the disciples at Pentecost (Ac 1:14).

Most especially, Mary is presented as the model of discipleship. In Mark 3:31–5 Jesus' family and his mother are contrasted with the crowd sitting round Jesus. They remain outside, while those around Jesus are complimented, 'Here are my mother and my brothers. Anyone who does the will of God, that person is my brother and sister and mother'. To this passage Luke makes a series of small but significant changes in 8:19–21, which must be regarded as deliberate: the contrast and the implied criticism are removed. His mother and brothers, 'came looking for him, but they could not get to him because of the crowd.' Jesus does not 'look at those sitting in a circle round him' (Mk 3:34) before declaring 'My mother and brothers are those who hear the word of God and put it into practice' (Lk 8:21): by implication he includes his mother and his brothers in the blessing. The passage is made more significant by its change of position: Luke places it immediately after a series of parables, so that Mary and his brothers are the first who hear his word and put it into practice.

Consequently, in a purely Lukan passage (11:27–8), when the woman in the crowd cries, 'Blessed the womb that bore you and the breasts that fed you!', the following blessing applies primarily and without any contrast to Mary's discipleship, 'More blessed still are those who hear the word of God and keep it'. It is, then, only fitting that Mary too should be present among the disciples at Pentecost.

3 LUKE AND THE POOR

Luke's attitude to poverty is somewhat complicated. He moves in a richer and more sophisticated world than Mark; he does not condemn this world, and shows some attitudes typical of it. At the same time he constantly points out the dangers of wealth, and the blessing of God on the poor. It may be precisely *because* he lives in a richer world, where inequality of wealth is more striking, that his message is so strong on this matter.

The two attitudes are reconciled by his insistence on the need for generosity in the matter of wealth and almsgiving. We will take each of these points in turn.

Luke's social position

Luke's considerably more sophisticated vocabulary and style of Greek, the elevated introductions to both his volumes in the style of Hellenistic historians, and his literary approach to his subject, all indicate a background and situation higher in the social scale than Mark, who writes a sort of kitchen-Greek, of the style spoken by slaves all around the Mediterranean world. It would never have entered Mark's head to address his audience with a literary preface.

In the Acts Luke is careful to show that Christianity is not confined exclusively to the lower classes, but included in its ranks Manaen, 'who had been brought up with Herod the tetrarch' (Ac 13:1) and Dionysius the Areopagite at Athens (17:34). Not only the higher sums of money mentioned, but also Luke's knowledge of finance, investment and banking point to a more leisured and affluent situation of himself and his audience.

It is an interesting social commentary that shame plays a greater part in Luke as a motive than in the other gospels: the Crafty Steward would be ashamed to beg (Lk 16:3); both the householder roused by a Friend at Midnight and the Unjust Judge are eventually forced into action by the desire to avoid public exposure. Luke is often at pains to point out the good repute of important characters (e.g. Ac 5:34; 6:3). There is an element of bourgeois respectability lurking in him.

The blessing of God on the poor

From the very first Luke stresses that Jesus came bringing God's blessing to the poor. Mary's canticle underlines in several different ways that God has now 'filled the starving with good things' (Lk 1:53). No house can be found for Jesus to be born in; he is welcomed by shepherds; in the Temple his parents make the offering of the poor. In line with this, the Opening Proclamation of Jesus at Nazareth, which forms the programme for his ministry, is a proclamation to the poor. Jesus takes as his text, 'he has anointed me to bring the good news to the afflicted . . . to let the oppressed go free' (4:18, quoting Isaiah 61:1–2).

Luke's version of the Beatitudes is especially instructive. Whereas Matthew's Beatitudes (Mt 5:2–12) are concerned with spiritual attitudes – 'poor *in spirit*', 'hunger and thirst *for justice*', 'pure *in heart*' – Luke's lack these qualifications. Of his four Beatitudes, three concern those who are actually afflicted, without any reference to their religious attitude; the poor, the hungry and those who weep. It is to these that the kingdom belongs and to these that it will bring relief. Only in the last of Luke's Beatitudes does any specifically religious note enter, to those who are outcasts 'on account of the Son of man'. Till then Luke has been pointing to a social, not a religious, class. This lesson is reinforced by the four 'woes' with which Luke balances the Beatitudes; here again it is a social class which is envisaged, or at least those who enjoy the pleasures and good repute of the world, without any clause excusing those who do so innocently: 'alas for you who are rich . . . who have plenty to eat now . . . who are laughing now . . . when everyone speaks well of you' (6:24–6).

Such is the lesson also of the parable of the Rich Man and Lazarus, especially when it is seen against the story which is its probable background. There is a Palestinian story about a poor scholar and a rich tax gatherer whose situations are reversed in heaven.[4] But when Luke adapts the story he not only refrains from saying anything about the merits of Lazarus and the faults of the rich man, he positively removes the built-in good qualities of the poor man (a scholar of the Law) and the bad qualities of the rich man (an unclean tax collector). It is the position itself of being rich or poor which determines the place in the next world.

What should the rich do?

Here Luke is not quite so clear. On the one hand he is insistent that following Christ involves total renunciation. In Mark and Matthew the first four disciples leave behind their nets or their boat and their father; it is only in Luke that they give up 'everything' (Lk 5:11). Likewise at the call of Levi, Luke is careful to state explicitly that the tax collector left 'everything' (5:28). Just so with the ruler (Matthew's rich young man) who wants to follow Jesus; he must sell 'everything' he has (18:22). Most absolute of all, Luke has Jesus proclaim, 'none of you can be my disciple without giving up all that he owns' (14:33), a passage unparalleled in other gospels. It is no doubt in fulfilment of this that the early community in Jerusalem held all their possessions in common (Ac 2:44–5).

On the other hand Luke does not always seem to demand this total renunciation. Zacchaeus gave only half his possessions to the poor (Lk 19:8). A man who has two tunics need give only a share, not both tunics, to the man who has none (3:11). In the Acts the crime of Ananias and Sapphira was not to keep back the money – this they were

---

[4] J. Sanh. 6.23c.

perfectly at liberty to do (Ac 5:4) – but to pretend falsely that they were giving all.

It is more that the situation of the rich is a dangerous one. The Pharisees are criticised because they love money (Lk 16:14), rather than for any dishonesty. In another passage they are even offered a clean bill of health: 'Give alms from what you have and, look, everything will be clean for you' (11:41). Perhaps the fiercest little vignette in the whole gospel is addressed to the rich man who planned to extend his barns to accommodate his increasing wealth: 'Fool! This very night the demand will be made for your soul; and this hoard of yours, whose will it be then?' (12:20). The dangerous situation can be redeemed only by generosity, as offered by the Good Samaritan, or as the Rich Man withholds from Lazarus. Frequent small touches show the importance of this lesson for Luke: at 6:30 he changes the tense so that the instruction reads, 'Give [habitually] to everyone who asks you'; and elsewhere, 'Sell your possessions and give to those in need' (12:33).

4 LUKE AND REPENTANT SINNERS

It is a striking fact that Luke does not expect those who follow Jesus to have earned their vocation by any previous merits or good conduct. On the contrary, it is almost necessary that they should have been sinners, and the first prerequisite is that they should recognise this. This is perhaps because he is concerned above all with the preaching of the gospel outside Israel, to those who were living a wholly unregenerate form of life. Luke conceives the gospel as bringing hope to the hopeless and acceptance to the outcast. But within Israel too conversion is the necessary precondition to following Jesus.

Luke's concentration on this theme in comparison to the other evangelists becomes clear firstly merely by the occurrence of two expressions:

- The phrase 'the forgiveness of sins' occurs in Mark only at 1:4, as part of John the Baptist's message, and in Matthew only at 26:29, in Jesus' words over the cup at the Last Supper: in Luke it occurs five times and in the Acts again five times.
- The word 'repentance' occurs once in Mark and twice in Matthew (all in the context of the ministry of John the Baptist); in Luke it is used five times and in Acts six times. Similarly, the verb 'to repent' occurs twice in Mark, five times in Matthew, but in Luke

nine times and in the Acts five times. Neither word occurs at all in John.

Mark and Matthew of course have the saying of Jesus, 'It is not the healthy who need the doctor, but the sick. I came to call not the upright, but sinners' (Mk 2:17; Mt 9:12–13), which Luke repeats (Lk 5:31–2). But in Luke it seems almost a necessary precondition for being called to be a sinner and to confess this fact. At the call of the first disciples in Mark and Matthew we hear nothing of their previous moral condition, but in Luke Peter proclaims, 'Leave me, Lord; I am a sinful man' (5:8) before Jesus calls and commissions him.

Similarly Matthew has the parable of the Two Sons (Mt 21:28–32), where the first son, who wins acceptance, initially refused to do his father's will. In Luke, however, there is the story of the Prodigal Son (possibly developed from Matthew's parable). Here the repentance of the prodigal younger son after his period as a wastrel explicitly wins acceptance by his repentance, while the dutiful elder son eventually forfeits all sympathy by his self-righteousness, his stubborn rudeness towards his father, and his spiteful malice towards his own brother (Lk 15:11–32). In like vein the lack of courtesy towards Jesus on the part of Simon the Pharisee, who needs to be 'forgiven little', contrasts painfully with the overflowing expression of love and repentance by the Woman who was a Sinner (7:36–50).

Again, Matthew has the parable of the Lost Sheep (18:12–13); in the context of the Discourse on the Church (Mt 18), the lesson here is the duty of the community to seek out the lost sheep. In Luke 15:4–10 this parable is doubled by that of the Lost Coin, and the lesson is subtly different: 'There will be more rejoicing in heaven over one sinner repenting than over ninety-nine upright people who have no need of repentance'. In Luke these two parables and the adjoining Prodigal Son all illustrate the complaint of the Pharisees and scribes, 'This man welcome sinners and eats with them' (15:2). There is no precondition of good behaviour, only of willingness to repent – as in the story of Zacchaeus (19:1–10). Perhaps the most forceful example of all is the story of the Good Thief (23:40–3): having first twice acknowledged their inexcusable guilt, he wins acceptance simply by turning to Jesus.

5 THE COMMUNITY OF SALVATION

Such, then, is Luke's community of salvation. It is not those to whom salvation was conventionally thought to be addressed, male Jews who obeyed the Law and walked complacently before the Lord. Israel is indeed not excluded from salvation, for the promises of God must be fulfilled. But the greater part of Israel have rejected their salvation, and they are to be replaced by a motley collection of outcasts, of physical and moral cripples, despised by society. Confronted with Jesus and his message, these people simply recognise their need and commit themselves to him as Saviour.

6 PERSONAL STUDY

1. Do you find Luke's Jesus too demanding or too indulgent? If not, why not?
2. Is Luke's message unfair on any class of people?

CHAPTER 14

LUKE'S PARABLES

Imagery is a prime means of driving home a lesson, not only among country people and primitives: international economics may be memorably analysed in terms of two boys selling ice-cream on a beach, or DNA in terms of a zip fastener. Every good preacher knows that a story may well remain in the minds of the listeners long after the message it carried has been forgotten, but that if the story is really apt the lesson it conveyed may also lodge in the minds of the hearers.

From ancient times myths have been used to convey lessons about the relationship of the world to God or to the gods, whether in Mesopotamia, Africa or the Bible. They have been used by philosophers to analyse reality (Plato's myth of the cave, or Wittgenstein's beetle in a box), as means of political satire (Jotham's Fable in Judges 9, Swift's *Gulliver's Travels* or Orwell's *1984*), and as a commentary on human behaviour (Adam and Eve, Aesop's *Fables*, or Graham Greene's novels). Country people particularly, as they spend large portions of their work and leisure time among animals, plants and organic growth, have often expressed the profound truths, the fruit of their reflections, in terms of those natural living things.

Christians regard the biblical stories and myths as inspired – that is, as conveying God's view and meaning. But the divine message is expressed in forms which are similar to the means used to convey other messages.

1 THE PARABLES OF JESUS IN MARK

In the Gospel of Mark Jesus uses both story parables and short images to convey his message. The two major stories of the Sower and the Wicked Tenants occur at the turning points of each half of the gospel. The former (4:1–8) is an image of Jesus' lack of success with the multitudes and his turning to instructing the disciples: most of the Sower's seed goes to waste, but some of it bears good fruit. The latter story (12:1–12), sandwiched between the challenge to Jesus' authority in the Temple and a group of Four Controversies with the leading groups of the Jews, is an image of the failure of the Jewish leaders to produce fruit from the vineyard of Israel. Besides these two longer stories there are also the short parable stories of the Mustard Seed and the Seed Growing Secretly (4:26–32).

The principles of form criticism have made clear that the original use of the parables was not necessarily that which they now illustrate in the gospel. Passages handed down separately in the oral tradition were at some time assembled 'like pearls on a string' – and, as Morna Hooker has pointed out, often with the skill and care with which pearls are arranged on a string. As the message of Jesus was passed on, this was done in the context of the cares and interests of the developing Christian community, and of its developing theology of Christ after the Resurrection.

The basic stories told by Jesus in Mark all concern the coming of the kingdom, which was the principal object of Jesus' teaching. They seem to have been replies either to criticism from outside or to puzzlement from inside. Thus the stories of the Mustard Seed and of the Seed Growing Secretly could both have been told originally to explain how the small and undistinguished group of Jesus' disciples could be posing as the realisation of God's kingdom. The sovereignty of God had been expected to break out in such a way that the whole world would be transformed; how could Jesus now be claiming that this motley little band represented such a transformation? The two longer stories also, the Sower and the Wicked Tenants, similarly concern the process of the coming of the kingdom. It is probable that the chief message of these parables of Jesus was the immediacy of the kingdom.[1] They are designed to spur the hearers on to appreciate that the moment has come and urging them to make a decision for Jesus.

---

[1] This is fully documented in the two classic treatments of the parables: C. H. Dodd, *The Parables of the Kingdom* (London, Nisbet, 1935), and J. Jeremias, *The Parables of Jesus* (tr. S. H. Hooke, London, SCM, 1972).

After the Passion and Resurrection, these simple images were adjusted to correspond more closely to the reality which had now happened. Thus Jesus used the biblical image of the wedding feast to describe the joys of the coming of the kingdom, the final wedding of God and his people of Israel. After his Passion Jesus himself was seen as the bridegroom, and the Passion was interpreted as his being taken away. So the parable could be adjusted: 'Surely the bridegroom's attendants cannot fast while the bridegroom is still with them? As long as they have the bridegroom with them, they cannot fast. But the time will come when the bridegroom is taken away from them and then, on that day, they will fast' (Mk 2:19–20). This tailpiece does not sit too happily on the original story: in the normal situation of a wedding, the bridegroom is not taken off in such a way that the revellers turn to mourning. On the other hand, it corresponds all too well to the situation of Jesus, and could aptly have been added after the Passion.

In the same way the image of the Sower sowing his seed, some successfully, some unsuccessfully, was interpreted in detail, a particular meaning being attached to each of the kinds of failure. The circumstances detailed fit the situation of the early Church and its mission far better than that of Jesus and his mission in Galilee. In Galilee there was little opportunity among Jesus' first disciples for 'the lure of riches', nor does there seem to have been persecution; these became a threat only after Pentecost in the early mission of the Church. Nor does the allegorical meaning fit too well onto the story: at first the seed is interpreted as the *Word* (a name given to the message of Jesus in the early preaching), while later in the interpretation it becomes the different *kinds of people* who receive the Word. The original parable fits well into Jesus' situation, and he could well have told it as an image of his lack of success with the crowds in Galilee, and the significant and fruitful success of his teaching to the Twelve. In this case the allegorical interpretation came about only during the mission of the Church.

Similarly the parable of the Seed Growing Secretly (4:26–9) may well have been extended by the early Church. Without the image of the

harvest in the final verse it would be, like the Mustard Seed, an image of the quiet coming of the kingdom, another crisis parable. The addition of the threat of harvest brings in a new dimension of a second moment, which was one of the interests of the early Church after the delay of the immediate second coming of Christ.

The parable of the Wicked Tenants (12:1–12) may or may not be another example: this story makes ample sense in the context of Jesus' mission. The image of Israel as a vineyard of the Lord was familiar from the Old Testament and the image of the leaders of Israel as unsatisfactory tenants would have struck a ready chord. It is, however, another matter whether Jesus would have extended the detail of this image to include the murder of the Son. This possibility cannot be excluded, since in at least one saying of Jesus he so describes himself: 'But as for that day or hour, nobody knows it, neither the angels in heaven, nor the Son; no one but the Father (Mk 13:32). The early Church is unlikely to have invented a saying which attributed ignorance to Jesus, and if he so referred to himself in one saying, he may also have used this designation in the parable. In this case the whole parable would be from Jesus, including the indication that he was to be violently rejected by the Jewish authorities.

It seems, then, that the parables of Jesus were extended, altered and reapplied by the earliest tradition, relating them to the early Church's own situation with regard to Jesus' message.

2 LUKE AND THE OTHER SYNOPTIC GOSPELS

The parables in Luke are as follows. (Those marked * appear also in Matthew; those marked † appear also in Mark.)

1. The Two Builders* (6:46–9)
2. The Playing Children* (7:31–5)
3. The Two Debtors (7:36–50)
4. The Sower*† (8:4–15)
5. The Good Samaritan (10:25–37)
6. The Friend at Midnight (11:5–10)
7. The Rich Fool (12:13–21)
8. The Watchful Servants*† (12:35–8)
9. The Burglar* (12:39–40)
10. The Servant in Authority* (12:41–6)
11. The Defendant* (12:58–9)
12. The Barren Fig Tree (13:6–9)

13. The Mustard Seed★† (13:18–19)
14. The Leaven★ (13:20–1)
15. The Closed Door★ (13:23–30)
16. The Wedding Guests (14:7–11)
17. The Great Feast★ (14:15–24)
18. The Tower Builder (14:25–30)
19. The Warring King (14:31–3)
20. The Lost Sheep★ (15:1–7)
21. The Lost Coin (15:8–10)
22. The Prodigal Son (15:11–32)
23. The Crafty Steward (16:1–13)
24. The Rich Man and Lazarus (16:19–31)
25. The Servant's Reward (17:7–10)
26. The Unjust Judge (18:1–8)
27. The Pharisee and the Tax Collector (18:9–14)
28. The Pounds★ (19:11–27)
29. The Wicked Tenants★† (20:9–19)

Of these twenty-nine story parables in Luke, nearly half occur also in Matthew. Attention will be devoted principally to those which occur only in Luke. They will be considered from two points of view, the origin of the parables and the use to which Luke puts them.

3 LUKE'S USE OF PARABLES

It has been seen that Mark uses the parables principally to illustrate the nature of the kingdom or kingship of God which Jesus came to bring. This corresponds to the use of these parables before him, though in several cases it appears that Mark has extended their meaning so that they apply also to the situation of the community for which he is writing.

Matthew uses parables overwhelmingly (though not exclusively) in connection with the final judgement at the Second Coming of Christ, which is in any case a major preoccupation of his. Thus he inserts into his main parable chapter a pair of parables as a warning about the need to prepare for the final judgement, the Tares and the Dragnet (Mt 13:24–30, 47–50), the message of these being that at present the kingdom includes the bad as well as the good, and this will all be sorted out at the judgement. He emphasises the incalculability of the final reward by the parable of the Labourers in the Vineyard (20:1–16). He adds to the parable of the Great Feast another, the Wedding Garment

(22:11–14), to stress the need to prepare for the final judgement by good works. He expands Mark's little parable at the conclusion of the eschatological discourse (Mk 13:33–7) into four major story parables to do with readiness for the judgement (the Burglar, the Servant in Authority, the Ten Wedding Attendants, and the Talents: Mt 24:42—25:30), before adding the striking parable of the Sheep and the Goats for the last judgement itself (25:31–46).

Luke, similarly, uses parables to illustrate important aspects of his message.

Repentance

Repentance – the awareness of one's need for forgiveness – is a key theme in Luke (see pages 147–8). Three parables in particular are used to illustrate it.

The Two Debtors

The Two Debtors (Lk 7:36–50) is a typically Lukan story, with wonderful characterisation. The woman's delicacy in not daring to approach Jesus from the front, in not saying a word, the generosity of her repentance, and Jesus' tact towards the woman in not interrupting her silent grief – all are character traits depicted with loving Lukan care. The financial dimension of the parable is also Lukan; he is familiar with debtors and repayment. The lively dialogue is particularly Lukan, including its final challenging question. It is, however, also notable that the parable indicates the lack of logic which is characteristic of Luke (see page 121): the parable illustrates the lesson for Simon the Pharisee that generous forgiveness breeds generous love, whereas the scene requires the lesson that generous love breeds generous forgiveness.

It is tempting to speculate about the origin of such stories, linguistically and theologically so characteristic of Luke. Here one may suppose that Luke has derived the anointing from the Anointing at Bethany (Mk 14:3–9), which he omits. In both cases the host is called Simon, and the anointing with myrrh takes place at table. But while the weeping over Jesus' feet is a lovely gesture of repentance, anointing his feet (at Bethany his *head* is anointed) is rather strange: instead of feeling clean, the resultantly sticky feet would collect dust.

The Lost Coin

The Lost Coin (Lk 15:8–10) is introduced by Luke, possibly to pair with Matthew's parable of the Lost Sheep (Lk 15:4–7). As we have seen, Luke often pairs male with female; here the owner of the lost sheep is male, the owner of the lost coin female. However, the lesson of the parable is subtly different from that of Matthew. In Matthew the parable is part of the Discourse on the Community and its duties (Mt 18); the emphasis is on the duty of the Christian to search out and find what was lost. For Luke, however, the emphasis is on the joy over the conversion of a sinner. Luke adds his own delightful features: the shepherd expresses his affectionate joy by putting the sheep on his shoulders, and gleefully invites the neighbours in to share the celebration. The widow does the same – after the busy and practical fuss over the lamp (presumably the dwelling had no source of daylight other than the door) and the sweeping.

The Prodigal Son

The Prodigal Son (Lk 15:11–32; see pages 120 and 148) is another parable in which the lesson of repentance is stressed, again with Luke's

delicacy of characterisation, and again possibly derived from Matthew, from the parable of the Two Sons (Mt 21:28–32).

Prayer

Luke stresses the need for prayer especially by showing Jesus at prayer on the occasion of the turning points of his ministry (see page 132). One particularly important indication of his concentration is in the account of the Prayer in Gethsemane (Lk 22:39–46). Here Luke simplifies the story from the triple prayer in Mark – although really the stress in Mark is on the triple return of Jesus to the disciples, to find that they have failed him yet again – to a single prayer. Luke shows his view of the incident by wrapping it in the command at beginning and end, 'Pray not to be put to the test' (22:40, 46). It is an example to disciples, to teach that they too should pray at moments of crisis and testing. He elaborates this lesson by various parables.

The Friend at Midnight

While Matthew's version of the Lord's Prayer (Mt 6:9–13) is carried on and backed up by emphasis on the need for forgiveness, Luke's version (Lk 11:2–4) is given in the context of the need for persistence in prayer. This is done by a typically Lukan parable, where he has the audacity to give a dubious figure as the equivalent of God, as in the Unjust Judge. As often in Luke, the central figure is a rounded, human character: the householder is full of excuses, and he does the right thing for the wrong reason, in this case possible shame, lest the whole locality hear the refused request, persistently, and (in the Greek) 'shamelessly', shouted out into the night, no doubt with repeated appeals to their friendship. Luke is amusingly conscious of human respect: the Crafty Steward would be ashamed to beg (Lk 16:3); the presumptuous Wedding Guest is demoted to his shame (14:9). By contrast, in the Acts Luke frequently points out the high standing of converts and the respect in which they are held.

The whole scene is wittily painted, with the suggestion that the

father of the household is at the inside of the single living-room, in the furthest place from the door, needing to climb over the lesser members of the household in order to get to the door. Did Luke engender this story from the simple saying 'Knock and the door will be opened to you' (11:9)? The features of the story certainly betray his characteristic imaginative powers.

The Unjust Judge

The Unjust Judge (Lk 18:1–8) is a typical Lukan parable, teaching perseverance in prayer. There is the little monologue by the chief character, reflecting on what he should do to get out of this difficult situation which is his own fault, just like the Rich Fool, the Prodigal Son or the Crafty Steward. Only in Luke is the chief character of parables a rogue, unjust but with a certain pragmatic realism which makes him not unattractive. And only Luke has these parables which do not so much illustrate the situation (as the Markan parables illustrate the presence of the kingdom) as encourage a particular kind of action – 'imperative rather than indicative', as Goulder describes them.[2]

Goulder also suggests that Luke has formed this parable from the rather different figure of the Lord as judge in Ecclesiasticus (Si 35:14–15)

> He does not ignore the orphan's supplication,
>   nor the widow's as she pours out her complaint.
> Do the widow's tears not run down her cheeks,
>   as she accuses the man who is the cause of them?

In both passages there are the widow and the judge, and in both the widow wins through by her perseverance in her plea. But Luke has remoulded the judge to be one of his own lively characters.

---

[2] M. Goulder, *Luke – A New Paradigm*, vol. 1 (Sheffield, Sheffield Academic Press, 1989), p. 101.

The Pharisee and the Tax Collector

In the Pharisee and the Tax Collector (Lk 18:9–14) Luke combines many of these themes. Tax collectors like Zacchaeus are by nature outcasts, and thus the object of Luke's special attention: no matter how roguish they are, all sinners need to do in order to win acceptance is repent, like the Prodigal Son, to acknowledge their fault and turn to the Lord. This is precisely the point of difference between the two characters, as in the Prodigal Son. As in that story, but more simply, the characters are painted with deft touches – the oily, complacent Pharisee and the simple, contrite tax collector.

Salvation of the gentiles

That salvation was offered by Jesus to the gentiles is a constant Lukan preoccupations (see pages 141–3). This is the meaning of his adjustments to Matthew's parable of the Wedding Feast in his own parable of the Great Feast (see page 142).

This dimension is most fully shown in the parable of the Good Samaritan (Lk 10:25–37). In the telling of this story the genius of Luke is fully at work. The elements may well be drawn from a verse in 2 Ch 28:15, where the story concerns captives in war:

> Men nominated for the purpose then took charge of the captives. From the booty they clothed all of those of them who were naked; they gave them clothing and sandals, provided them with food and drink, mounted on donkeys all those who were infirm and took them back to Jericho . . . Then they returned to Samaria.

Booty, tending and clothing those in dire need, mounting on a donkey, the mention of Jericho and Samaria – all are elements which Luke has used in his story for a different purpose. The delicately-painted warmth and care of the Samaritan is very different from the impersonal, stock, black-and-white characteristics of the figures in Matthew's parables, who have only enough personality to contrast with each other. There

is also wit in the Samaritan's caution with money: he does not stint the innkeeper, but does not hand over unlimited funds either. The innkeeper will have to make out a case for further payment! A further element of wit might be evident to an audience familiar with Jewish ritual: the priest and the Levite would be rendered unclean, and so debarred from their ritual duties (and salary!), if the crumpled and abandoned victim turned out to be dead and so a defiling corpse. Theirs is a real dilemma, balancing the claims of neighbourliness against those of ritual correctness.

The cost of discipleship

Writing as he does for a comfortable society, Luke's concern for the poor and his awareness of the dangers of wealth present his audience with a real challenge (see pages 144–7).

The Rich Fool

The stark parable of the Rich Fool (Lk 12:13–21) presents the challenge uncompromisingly; it is one of the four imperative parables in Luke, encouraging action rather than merely describing a situation (the others being the Good Samaritan, the Rich Man and Lazarus, and the Pharisee and the Tax Collector). There is little room here for storytelling, but Luke still manages to present his anti-hero in a lifelike and witty manner, complete with a little monologue about how he should get out of his comfortably tiresome situation of superfluity. The lip-smacking self-

preoccupation is expressed in his referring to himself twelve times in three verses!

> 'What am *I* to do? *I* have not enough room to store *my* crops.' Then he said, 'This is what *I* will do: *I* will pull down *my* barns and build bigger ones, and store all *my* grain and *my* goods in them, and *I* will say to *my* soul: *My* soul, *you* . . .'
>
> (Lk 12:17–19, *italics added*)

This is followed by the typically Lukan four-barrelled salvo, 'take things easy, eat, drink, have a good time', just like the four different barrels in 14:21, 'the poor, the crippled, the blind and the lame', or in 21:16, 'parents and brothers, relations and friends'.

Is this parable another scintillating Lukan creation from two sources, an idea from one and an image from another? A closely similar idea comes in Ecclesiasticus (Si 11:18–20):

> Others grow rich by pinching and scraping,
>   and here is the reward they receive for it:
> although they say, 'Now I can sit back
>   and enjoy the benefit of what I have got,'
> they do not know how long it will last;
>   they will have to leave their goods to others and die.

The image of gathering into barns as storehouses of wealth as a process which distracts from the kingdom may be suggested by Matthew's birds in the sky, who 'do not sow or reap or gather into barns' (Mt 6:26).

The Wedding Guests

At more or less the mid-point of Jesus' great journey to Jerusalem, Luke introduces a whole series of parables about discipleship. The first two of these are linked by the theme of feasting, and are introduced by a story of a healing at a Sabbath meal (Lk 14:1–6).

Keeping the Sabbath

This story has striking similarities with an earlier story, given also by Mark and Matthew (Lk 6:6–11, cf. Mt 12:9–14 and Mk 3:1–6). In each story the Pharisees are malignantly watching Jesus. In each Jesus questions them whether it is lawful to heal on the Sabbath. Matthew shows Jesus giving as his authority for infringing the law a rabbinic legal *a fortiori* argument about a sheep falling into a pit or trench on the Sabbath. This Luke reserves for the later story, and then strengthens it to make it more dramatic and obviously urgent; he has a son or an ox fall into a well (hence the rush: Luke adds 'pull him out . . . without any hesitation'). The trench or pit is suitable enough, but I doubt whether it would be easy to find a well in Palestine which an ox could easily fall into! The watery well is also more nicely parallel to the man's watery disease of dropsy.

Luke then uses the scene of the meal to introduce his first two parables, the Wedding Guests and the Great Feast. Each teaches a characteristically Lukan message, but they are connected to each other more by the theme of guests at a feast than by their message.

The first parable is on humility, or knowing one's place, a condition of discipleship. This is an important quality; the Pharisee and the Tax Collector suggests that it is important perhaps especially as a precondition of repentance.

As the Rich Fool is related to a saying in the Wisdom literature, this parable similarly may well be based on Proverbs 25:6–7:

> do not take a place among the great;
> better to be invited, 'Come up here',
> than be humiliated in the presence of the prince.

Luke makes much of this motif of shame and honour: his characters are certainly not above doing the right thing for the wrong reason! So the Crafty Steward is prevented by shame from relying on begging; the Friend at Midnight gets what he wants by shouting out shamelessly and so shaming his friend (see pages 145, 157). Likewise, the incautious Tower Builder is made fun of (Lk 14:29). Here Luke builds on the model in Proverbs, painting both humiliation and honour with characteristic liveliness.

The Great Feast

The second party parable, the Great Feast (Lk 14:15–24), teaches an important lesson about the composition of the kingdom. On the characterisation, see page 121. The parable is preceded by a sort of heading (vv. 12–14), which it is partly intended to illustrate. The lesson of the heading is about human behaviour, the lesson of generosity to the underprivileged without hope of reward that is so much stressed by Luke (e.g. 6:32–5). It has many Lukan characteristics: one of his quartets (the poor, the crippled, the blind and the lame), the same stress on actual poverty as his Beatitudes, the same theme of parties.

The same lesson is carried on into the parable. This is based on Matthew's parable of the Wedding Feast (Mt 22:2–14), but discards both the wedding element and the king, not to mention the highly Matthean warning at the end about the need for good works (represented by the wedding garment). It is also a good deal more lifelike than the Matthean parable. Luke discards the artificiality of all the potential guests living in the same town, which can then be sacked by the army of the overreacting king: in Matthew this was surely an allegorical element, illustrating God's retribution against Jerusalem. Luke, as usual, makes lively characters. In Matthew one party of the invited guests simply goes off without a care, while the other party overreacts or allegorises by humiliating and killing the innocent messengers. In contrast to these wooden reactions, Luke's characters do at least have the courtesy to make a rich variety of excuses about supposedly pressing duties.

The most important change, however, is that Luke radically alters the meaning of the parable. In Matthew, especially coming as it does immediately after the parable of the Wicked Tenants, it reinforces the lesson of that parable, showing the bankruptcy and doom of Israel. In Luke this lesson is eclipsed by the emphasis on his favoured quartet of the poor, the crippled, the blind and the lame of the city – that is, the neglected of Israel. This lesson is the same as the emphasis throughout the Infancy Stories on the coming of salvation to the poor of Israel. But then Luke extends it by the second mission of the servant beyond the city to 'the open roads and the hedgerows', indicating the urgent call to other nations.

The Tower Builder and the Warring King

The full severity of Luke's teaching on commitment comes finally in the conclusion to these two parables (Lk 14:28–33). They start with the frequent Lukan challenge, 'which of you . . .?' (cf. 11:5, 15:4), and again there is the favourite Lukan motivation of shame, as the improvident Tower Builder is made fun of (see page 145). The seriousness of the

decision is, however, in each case pointed by the unusual action of *sitting down* to calculate the cost; usually Luke's characters are marked by their energetic activity, not by repose!

But it is the conclusion which is most striking, going beyond anything hitherto demanded. Luke has already warned, 'Sell your possessions and give to those in need . . . For wherever your treasure is, that is where your heart will be too' (12:33–4), and has stressed that the disciples called by Jesus leave *everything* behind. But here he makes total renunciation an absolute condition of discipleship. This goes beyond even what he represents in the ideal early Jerusalem community of Acts. A further threat is posed by the following little parable on salt, which suggests that those who fail to do this are like useless salt, good for nothing (14:34–5).

The Crafty Steward

This story (Lk 16:1–13) has often been considered the most scandalous of the parables, as though Luke were commending dishonesty, since the steward's master approves his action. This is to misread Luke's delight in a good story, to treat the story like an allegory (in which the master stands for God), and to neglect the clear moral given at the end: 'For the children of this world are more astute in dealing with their own kind than are the children of light.'

The story may find its origin in Matthew's story of the master with two servants who are debtors (Mt 18:23–35). But it would certainly have undergone a transformation; apart from the three main personalities there is little in common between the two stories. It is again typical of

Luke to give us such lively characters: the master accepts with a good grace what he cannot alter, perhaps even with a laugh; once the bills are changed, there is nothing he can do. Anyway, it was his own fault for not dismissing the steward summarily, but giving him time to take evasive action! Any audience would be amused first by the misery, then by the wit of the steward. The misery is depicted through one of those little Lukan soliloquies of his parable hero, complete with deliberative question, 'what am I to do?' (see page 158). Again there is the Lukan motive of shame, 'Go begging? I should be too ashamed.' Then his quick and crooked wit reasserts itself, as he calls his master's debtors one by one, so that each thinks he is receiving a unique favour, and with a smarmy courtesy.

How could he get away with it? One interpretation, careful that the steward should not be commended for this particular piece of dishonesty, holds that he is simply deducting his own commission for the deal. Another suggests that he is deducting the interest due to the master (oil was more easily adulterated than corn with a cheaper substance, so that a standard rate of interest was 50 per cent, whereas with corn it was only 25 per cent). Since lending at interest was forbidden by the Law, he is only making his master obey the Law – a nice piece of gerrymandering, which would especially delight an oriental audience. The rueful master could hardly complain at being forced to observe the Law!

The real lesson of the story, then, is only that the disciple needs to use money for the purposes of discipleship with as much seriousness and good sense as those who use it for other purposes.

The Rich Man and Lazarus

The same demand in discipleship for generosity, and the warning of the dangers of wealth, are represented eschatologically in the parable of the Rich Man and Lazarus (Lk 16:19–31). See page 146.

Luke's parables

It is in the parables that Luke's genius for storytelling, visible also elsewhere, is most memorable. The stories are thoroughly moulded in his style and suited to his purposes. Sometimes it is possible to discern a possible origin for the stories, in other gospels or elsewhere, but so thoroughly has Luke formed them that it is no longer possible to decide on their origin, or whether and how many of them he received from the oral tradition, from Jesus or via Jesus.

---

5 PERSONAL STUDY

1. Did Luke draw his parables from Jesus, from elsewhere, or from his own imagination?
2. What consequences has your answer for the inspiration of the New Testament?

CHAPTER 15

THE PASSION STORY IN LUKE

In all the gospels the Passion story is in some way the climax for which the whole of the rest of the story has served as an introduction. In Luke this is made plain particularly by two preliminary features, the theme of necessity and the great journey.

The death of their leader as a despised criminal, executed in the most humiliating way possible was, as Paul points out, a scandal, 'to the Jews an obstacle they cannot get over, to the gentiles foolishness' (1 Co 1:23). Our modern stylised crucifixes give little hint of the distress and shame of the event. In the ancient world, when people were familiar with what crucifixion was really like, no attempt was made at a realistic representation: crosses had no figure on them. Indeed the flight from reality was such that crosses were bejewelled, to escape from the grisly fact.

It was the earliest task of Christian apologetics to explain how this shame was necessary, and this could only be because God willed it so. The theme of the necessity of the Crucifixion, that everything is moving inexorably to this climax, hangs over the gospel from the start (see page 44), even as early as Simeon's prophecy of the sword to pierce Mary's heart. The concentration of nearly half the gospel on the great journey (see page 134), culminating in Jesus' death as a prophet at Jerusalem, also serves to focus on this event and its divinely willed inevitability: it is his *exodus* at Jerusalem, foreseen and faced up to at the Transfiguration (Lk 9:31).

Inevitably, of course, Luke treats each incident of the Passion in his own particular way.

1 ON THE MOUNT OF OLIVES

The Markan account

In Mark the emphasis of the incident (Mk 14:32–42, cf. Lk 22:39–46) is on the desertion of their Master by the disciples (see pages 88–9): It is the climax of their waywardness and unreliability. Three times Jesus returns from his prayer to find them sleeping, unable to share with him his acute distress. After the Agony comes the Arrest, and there too the accent is on the betrayal by the disciples.

The Lukan account

By a few delicate touches Luke gives a wholly new sense to the scene on the Mount of Olives. In his prayer Jesus gives an example to his followers, of how to pray in a time of testing. In the scene of the Arrest (Lk 22:47–53) the disciples offer Jesus their support, and it is only after he has offered Judas the opportunity to repent and has refused and remedied the violent support of the disciples that he allows the guards to arrest him.

The prayer of Jesus

Instead of Mark's three prayers (or more accurately, three returns, for Mark has little to say about the second prayer and none at all about the third), Luke gives only one prayer of Jesus. This is bracketed by the command, 'Pray not to be put to the test'. Not only does this command form a bracket in verses 40 and 46, and so give the sense of the incident, but also the whole incident is delicately composed on a symmetrical chiasmus:

  a Pray not to be put to the test
    b He withdrew from them
      c Kneeling down
        d Father, if you are willing
          e Take this cup away from me
        d' Let your will be done
      c' Standing up
    b' He went to his disciples
  a' Pray not to be put to the test

When Jesus taught them the Lord's Prayer he also gave them an example of prayer; similarly now he gives them the example of how a Christian should act in time of testing. He kneels down, as Christians do in fervent prayer (Ac 9:40, 20:36, 21:5), and stresses both before and after the central petition that the asking is subject to the Father's will.

The support of the disciples

The support of the disciples is stressed, and – so far as possible – their failure excused. When Jesus comes to them he finds them sleeping, indeed, but 'for sheer grief', so that even their sleep can be construed as a participation with Jesus. When it comes to the arrest, they are all eagerness: the unnamed sword-wielder is noted as one of his followers; they might well have continued the fight if Jesus had not restrained them! There is no mention of flight; on the contrary, at the Cross 'all his friends' stood there (Lk 23:49). Supported by Jesus, they in their turn support him.

The dignity of Jesus

Jesus himself is in control of the situation, and shows a calm dignity throughout, remaining true to himself. There is none of the abandonment of Mark's 'he began to feel terror and anguish' (Mk 14:34) and the thrice-repeated prayer. Jesus kneels down to pray, and prays 'more fervently'. Raymond Brown[1] plausibly interprets his 'agony' as related to the *agon* or contest of athletes, and explains the sweat-like drops of blood (Lk 22:44) as evidence of the pumping of adrenalin as Jesus tenses himself for the great contest. Jesus then stands erect as the arresting-party approaches, and encourages the disciples to do the same. As Judas approaches to kiss him, he greets his betrayer affectionately by name, and – he who has so often offered repentance to sinners – by his challenging question offers Judas one last chance to repent. He who has healed so many during his ministry heals now the servant whose ear had been cut off, and by his touch (another delicate gesture of Luke's). It is only when Jesus has signified his assent – 'But this is your hour; this is the reign of darkness' – that they can seize him.

2 IN THE HIGH PRIEST'S HOUSE

The Markan account

Mark's theological interests are here, as elsewhere, paramount (Lk 22:54–71; cf. Mk 14:53–72 – see pages 89–91). Some major emphases are:

1. The contrast between Jesus' firm stance before the High Priest and Peter's feeble triple denial of his Master. The contrast is brought out

---

[1] Raymond Brown, *The Death of the Messiah* (London, Geoffrey Chapman, 1994), p. 189.

by the Markan technique of sandwiching Jesus' steadfastness between the two halves of the scene of Peter's denial.

2. The triple accusation of Jesus and its Christological implications.

3. The scene as Mark presents it may well be a construction (by Mark, or possibly by the tradition on which he drew) to highlight the two reasons which led to Jesus' arrest and condemnation.

The Lukan account

Luke makes considerable alterations to the material which he received from Mark.

Peter's denial of Jesus

Peter's denial is no longer placed on either side of Jesus' steadfast affirmation. It is no part of Luke's theology to stress Peter's guilt by means of the contrast between Peter and Jesus. Instead, Luke places Peter's denial before the meeting of the council, which does not take place until morning.

This may be a historical correction, to locate the council session at a more probable time, and meanwhile to fill up the night. But it has also a typically Lukan theological motivation. As soon as Peter has denied his Master for the third time, Jesus turns and looks at Peter (they must therefore have been in the same room) and so brings him to repentance. For the second time in the Passion Narrative Jesus offers repentance, this time to be accepted.

The mockery of Jesus by the guards

The mockery by the guards is also placed by Luke in the night-time vacated by his transfer of the council meeting to the morning. The emphasis is less on the physical maltreatment with blows than on the mockery, challenging Jesus to divine who struck him. This 'blind man's buff' corresponds roughly to several blindfold guessing-games current at the time. The emphasis on making fun of Jesus occurs twice more, in the mockery of Jesus by Herod (Lk 23:11) and by the soldiers at the Cross (23:36). It reflects Luke's sensitivity to shame (see pages 145 and 157).

It is also significant that the guards mock Jesus specifically as a prophet. In Mark this was no doubt seen as mockery of the claim Jesus had just made that they would see 'the Son of man seated at the right hand of the Power', and so on. In Luke, however, the interrogation at which this claim occurs has not yet taken place. The mockery as a prophet therefore must be seen to bear on Jesus' whole ministry, in which Luke especially represents him as a prophet (see pages 133–5). It is of course as a prophet that Luke has told us that Jesus is to meet his end at Jerusalem.

The interrogation of Jesus

The interrogation itself has changed character in Luke. There is no mention of the High Priest, nor of Jesus' saying about the Temple. This is because Luke's whole attitude to Jesus in the Temple is different from that of Mark. The Temple has played an important part in the gospel right from the Infancy Stories onwards, and will play an important part in the Jerusalem community in the early part of Acts. So in Jesus' Jerusalem ministry the Temple has a different role from its role in Mark and in Matthew. In those gospels Jesus is seen as demonstrating that the Temple is now obsolete and must be swept away; in Luke the Temple is the centre of his royal and messianic activity of teaching, just as it will be the centre of the early Christian community in Jerusalem, and the centre to which Paul constantly returns and where Paul teaches:

1. Jesus enters Jerusalem as king. At the great entry into Jerusalem, whereas in Mark the crowds hail 'the coming kingdom of David our father' (Mk 11:10) in Luke they cry 'Blessed is he who is coming as King in the name of the Lord' (Lk 19:38). This is further stressed by the unsuccessful attempt of the Pharisees to silence the crowd, astonishingly addressing Jesus as 'teacher' (19:39–40), an address given to Jesus regularly during the Jerusalem ministry (21:7).
2. Far from sweeping the Temple away, Jesus uses it as his centre for daily teaching. The fact that he 'taught in the Temple every day' (19:47) is the climax to which the 'Cleansing' scene leads. Jesus' teaching brackets the whole Jerusalem ministry, occurring here at the beginning of it and later (21:37), at the end. So the objection of the authorities and their challenge to his authority concerns, in Luke, not any destructive action but his teaching and evangelising: it is when he has been shown teaching and preaching the Good News in the Temple that they challenge him, 'what authority have you for acting like this?' (20:1–2 – a challenge which in Mark refers to his demonstration *against* the Temple).

Furthermore, the scene cannot any longer be called a 'trial'. Goulder[2] qualifies it as 'a kangaroo court' in Luke. There is no evidence and no verdict, and indeed when they bring Jesus before Pilate they merely accuse him as though this scene had never occurred. At the Jewish

[2] M. Goulder, *Luke – A New Paradigm*, vol. 2 (Sheffield, Sheffield Academic Press, 1989), p. 753.

interrogation Jesus is in control; the leaderless group of 'elders . . . chief priests and scribes' is no more than a foil to Jesus, enabling him to make two separate confessions or claims; that he is the Christ and that he is the Son of God. Whereas in Mark and Matthew Jesus is silent (as the Suffering Servant of Isaiah), in Luke he testifies on his own behalf, so that his own witness gives his opponents their impetus: and they stress (by subtle changes by Luke to the emphasis of the expression), 'Why do we need any evidence? We have heard it ourselves from his own lips' (22:71).

Each of the two claims made receives a new prominence.

1. *That Jesus is the Christ* First of all, the authorities no longer merely ask Jesus whether he is the Christ: they demand that he proclaim it, 'If you are the Christ, tell us.' Then Luke points out the futility of any attempt to convince the authorities: 'If I tell you, you will not believe, and if I question you, you will not answer' – a resignation reminiscent of Abraham's rejection of the Rich Man's plea in the parable: 'If they will not listen either to Moses or to the prophets, they will not be convinced even if someone should rise from the dead' (Lk 16:31). As in the Pilate scene the stress will be on the Jewish determination to have Jesus executed, so here it is on the stubbornness of Jesus' interrogators, and their refusal to accept the truth.

From the Christological point of view the importance is that Luke significantly alters Jesus' own interpretation of 'Christ'. To the Markan claim – immediately denounced by the High Priest as blasphemy – that they will see the Son of man sharing the awesome chariot-throne of God, Luke makes two changes:

– It is no longer a matter of sight and in the future. It is a matter of fact and vividly present: not 'you will see', but 'from now on, the Son of man will be seated . . .'.
– There is no 'coming with the clouds of heaven'. The interest is no longer in the Second Coming or the final judgement. As the Second Coming has continued to delay, Luke's interest has moved from the future to the present: the emphasis is not on the future coming but on the present exaltation of Christ.

So the Son of man is presented as entering his glory now, and ready at the right hand of God to receive his faithful, just as he will be ready to welcome the first martyr, Stephen, who sees 'the heaven thrown open . . . and the Son of man standing at the right hand of God' (Ac 7:56). Throughout the Passion Narrative, Luke is aware of the dimension of Jesus in his Passion supporting his followers in theirs.

2. *That Jesus is the Son of God* This title is no longer joined to that of Christ, but receives a separate value of its own, in accordance with Luke's more developed understanding of the Lordship of Christ. Similarly at the Annunciation the child is separately predicted as Christ and as Son of God. What is most significant is that *all* Jesus' opponents confess this dignity of Jesus: 'They all said, "So you are the Son of God then?" He answered, "It is you who say I am." '

3 BEFORE PILATE AND HEROD

In the case of Jesus before Pilate and Herod (Lk 23:1–25) it is not necessary first to detail the procedure of the Markan account (see pages 91–2), for Luke's version is not radically different in orientation. It does, however, have some emphases which are not present in Mark's version.

The persecution of Jesus
Luke is always keen to align the persecution of Jesus with that of his followers, to show that Jesus underwent the same trials, and to stress that he therefore stands beside his followers in theirs. This is the dominant motif behind the Herod incident. Similarly in Paul's trials, he is taken first before the Roman governor, and then before the Jewish king, Herod Agrippa II. Herod Antipas, before whom Jesus appears, is not, it is true, a king; but as tetrarch he plays the same role. Historically, the referral of Jesus to the ruler of Galilee is not improbable: as an ostentatiously pious Jew, Herod might well have made the pilgrimage to Jerusalem for the feast, and at this time according to Roman law a prisoner could be judged in the *forum delicti* or the *forum domicilii* – that is, either where the supposed crime had been committed or where his domicile was (in the case of Jesus, Galilee). If Pilate wished to be rid of the case, it would have been a neat ploy to refer the prisoner to Herod.

It is hard to resist the impression that Herod, with typical Lukan vivacity, is represented as a rather wacky character. His reaction to having Jesus sent to him is excessive: ἐχάρη λίαν (literally 'he was too overjoyed', Lk 23:8) almost suggests whoops of joy. The same slightly maniacal overtone is given by the interrogation λόγοις ἱκανοῖς ('at sufficient length', Lk 23:9); there is a hint of excess here. Then, frustrated at Jesus' silence, Herod (to translate literally) 'makes nothing of him' and descends to the indignity of joining his soldiery in this play-acting mockery. The same hysterical bonhomie is suggested by the reconciliation thereby effected with Pilate (23:12).

Luke's care for history

Another emphasis of Luke in the account is a care for history. This appears in two details.

1. Mark gives us no details of any charge preferred against Jesus before Pilate; Pilate just somehow seems to know that Jesus claims to be king of the Jews. Luke shows Jesus' captors giving definite charges. They are, of course, false; but they are the sort of charges which could have been brought against Jesus on this occasion: subverting the people, preventing the payment of tribute to Caesar, and claiming to be Christ, a king. They are also similar to the charges preferred against Paul at Thessalonika: turning the whole world upside down, breaking Caesar's edicts, claiming that there is another king, Jesus (Ac 17:6–7).

2. Luke is considerably more cautious than Mark about the Barabbas incident. There is no mention in Luke of any amnesty or regular custom of releasing a prisoner – a Markan detail (Mk 15:6) which is not attested in external history, and which may well be an unjustified Markan deduction. According to Luke the crowd simply roar for the release of Barabbas, and are not to be put off by the offer of the release of Jesus. The contrast is all the stronger between Jesus, unjustly accused of subverting the people, and Barabbas, who had in fact been involved in a riot and bloodshed.

Pilate's recognition of the innocence of Jesus

Luke's chief emphasis is, however, on Pilate's recognition of the innocence of Jesus. Three times Pilate declares that he can find no case against this man, and three times the Jewish authorities insist on pressing their case. With each declaration of Jesus' innocence Pilate embraces a wider circle, first the charge which has been made, then any charge, and finally any evil at all:

- v. 4: ' "I find no case against this man." But they persisted . . .'
- v. 14: ' "I have . . . found no grounds in the man for any of the charges you bring against him . . ." But as one man they howled . . .'
- v. 22: ' "But what harm has this man done? I have found no case against him that deserves death . . ." But they kept on shouting at the top of their voices . . .'

It is only in Luke that Pilate first (in the Greek text of v. 16) suggests that he whip Jesus (a lighter punishment than the flogging of Mark and Matthew), and then actually wants to release him (v. 20). Finally Luke again stresses the responsibility of the Jewish leaders: Pilate 'handed Jesus over to them to deal with as they pleased' (v. 25). The execution is not Pilate's will. He pronounces no sentence; indeed, it is even as though the Jews rather than the Romans actually carried out the execution.

This emphatic insistence that the Roman authorities could find no case against Jesus is again probably to be seen in the light of the later history of the Church: Luke wishes to show that in Roman eyes Christianity is harmless and deserves no persecution.

4 ON CALVARY

The evangelists delay little on the details of the Crucifixion; their purpose is not to describe but to interpret this barbaric and humiliating death (Lk 23:26–49; cf. Mk 15:21–41 – see pages 93–5). In Luke's account, just as he did at the Arrest, Jesus remains in dignified control throughout. Moreover, the support he receives from others is striking, making it almost a triumphal progress: on the way to the Crucifixion he is supported by three different parties, Simon, the women and the criminals. After his death again support comes from three parties, the centurion, the crowds and the disciples. There is no cry of dereliction, but instead Jesus dies only when he has signified his readiness by commending his spirit to God.

Throughout his ministry Jesus has brought people to repentance and offered them forgiveness. Such a ministry reaches its climax at Calvary; there the Saviour completes his mission, and accordingly offers salvation to all those with whom he comes in contact. It is a scene of repentance and reconciliation.

1. The road to Calvary is dominated by the mourning and repentance of 'large numbers of people' and 'the daughters of Jerusalem' (Lk 23:27–8). Here Luke uses the word for 'people' which indicates not merely crowds but the Chosen People, the People of God. It is, then, as representatives of Israel that both these groups express their sorrow.
2. Even as the executioners are engaged on their gruesome task Jesus forgives them – as Stephen will do at his martyrdom (Ac 7:60). Jesus' forgiveness is again the model for that of his disciples.
3. The Good Thief turns to Jesus and earns his forgiveness by simply acknowledging his guilt. This he does twice: 'in our case we deserved it: we are paying for what we did.' In Luke turning to Jesus with the admission of sin is the unique way to salvation (see pages 147–9).

4. The centurion also acknowledges Jesus, not only by recognising him as 'upright', but by giving glory to God. Elsewhere in Luke this is the reaction of someone who has been miraculously cured by Jesus or of the crowds who witness it (5:25, 26; 7:16; 13:13; 17:15; 18:43); it is a full acknowledgement that God is at work in Jesus.

5. Finally the death of Jesus occasions a general movement of repentance: 'when all the crowds who had gathered for the spectacle saw what had happened, they went home beating their breasts' (23:48).

In sharp contrast to this turning to Jesus is the reaction of the leaders, the soldiers and the other thief. Ironically they taunt the Saviour with being unable to save himself, each time sharpening the taunt and the irony by the focus of a title:

— the leaders (pointedly distinguished from 'the people', who merely stood there watching): 'let him save himself, if he is the Christ of God, the Chosen One';
— the soldiers: 'If you are the king of the Jews, save yourself';
— the thief: 'Are you not the Christ? Save yourself'.

The irony of their taunts is all the sharper in that Luke is the evangelist who most thinks of Jesus as the Saviour.

Salvation

Apart from Luke (twice in the gospel, twice in Acts) only John 4:42 calls Jesus 'Saviour'. Similarly 'salvation' frequently in Luke describes God's work in Jesus (six times in Luke, seven times in Acts); otherwise only John 4:22.

Immediately after the death of Jesus the lie is given to the disbelief of this trio by the trio of supporters, the centurion, the crowds and the disciples.

5 PERSONAL STUDY

1. Compare the two Passion Narratives of Mark and Luke, underlining changes made by Luke. (This can most easily be done if you have the two gospels open, parallel, before you.)

2. Write an essay: 'In what way does Luke's message about the Passion differ from Mark's?'

CHAPTER 16

THE INFANCY NARRATIVE

It may seem strange to discuss the first two chapters of the gospel at such a late stage. The Infancy Narrative is the introduction to the story, and all introductions are written last, when the author knows exactly what is to be introduced! In this case, particularly, the introduction is not given by Mark, so that clearly Luke is working independently of his principal source for the main part of the gospel. The principal purpose both of Matthew and of Luke in their Infancy Narratives is to show that the Jesus of the ministry, presented by Mark, had already from his very inception and birth the qualities which became clear in the course of the ministry. Luke's account is, therefore, a prime source for understanding how he sees Jesus.

1 THE SHAPE OF THE STORY

The significance of Jesus is shown strongly by a comparison with the Annunciation and Birth of John the Baptist. John is shown to be the fulfilment of the hopes of Israel; Jesus is shown to be yet more. The two children are presented in parallel:

John	*Jesus*
The annunciation of John (1:5–25)	The Annunciation of Jesus (1:26–38)
The Visitation (1:39–56)	
The Birth of the Baptist (1:57)	The Birth of Jesus (2:6)
The visit of the neighbours (1:58)	The visit of the shepherds (2:8–20)

The Circumcision and Naming (1:59–65)	The Circumcision and Naming (2:21)
The child's future (1:66)	The child's future (2:33)
The canticle of the father (1:67–79)	The canticle of the mother (1:46–55)
The growth of the child (1:80)	The growth of the child (2:52)

Of these parallels, of course, the most important are those of the two Annunciations and the two Births.

2 THE ANNUNCIATIONS

While Matthew uses a formula-quotation at the end of each episode of his Infancy Narrative, to show that the events fulfil the promises of the Old Testament, Luke uses a more extensive allusive method. The whole atmosphere of the Infancy Narratives is redolent of the Old Testament, showing that the events stand within that tradition and that we are witnessing its completion. The parents of John are 'upright in the sight of God' and impeccable in carrying out the demands of the Law; Zechariah is a priest offering incense; Mary is the perfect representative of the poor of Yahweh so favoured in the Old Testament. The spirituality of the Old Testament is particularly clear in the canticles of Zechariah and Mary; Mary and Joseph are almost over-eager to fulfil the demands of the Law at the presentation (by the Law only the mother, not both parents, need be purified); and the story begins and ends in the Temple at Jerusalem.

Artist of language as he is, Luke enhances this atmosphere by the biblical language he uses. Thus the repeated phrase 'now it happened that . . .' is a frequent formula of the Greek Bible. The parallelism and balance of phrases ('The Holy Spirit will come upon you' with 'and the power of the Most High will cover you with its shadow'; 'Of all women you are the most blessed' with 'and blessed is the fruit of your womb') is characteristic of Hebrew poetry (see page 122).

At the same time the atmosphere of the early Church is apparent. Luke wishes to show that the beginnings of the story of Jesus are similar to those of the story of the Church. The outpouring of the Spirit on all the participants in the story (1:15, 41, 67, 80; 2:25–7) is reminiscent of the guidance by the Spirit of every movement of the early Church. The attendance of angels is also reminiscent of their repeated presence in the Acts. Finally, the parallel between the Baptist and Jesus is balanced by that in the Acts between Peter and Paul.

Especially significant is the fact that both Annunciation stories are

narrated in such a way as to bring out the similarity with annunciations of miraculous births in the Old Testament. The closest models to the Annunciation to Zechariah are the promise to Samson's mother (Jg 13:2–7) and the promise to Samuel's mother (1 S 1). In both of these the child is to be dedicated to the Lord and is not to drink wine or strong drink. In the latter the promise is also the answer to prayer in the sanctuary. But there are similarities also with the promise to Abraham and Sarah (Gn 18:10), both of whom are advanced in years beyond the age of parenthood.

On the other hand a quite new note is struck by the naming of Gabriel. This gives an eschatological aspect to the promise, for Gabriel appears to Daniel 'at the hour of the evening sacrifice' (Dn 9:21) to explain to him the promise of the Seventy Weeks, which concerns the coming of the Anointed Prince and the liberation of Israel. The same eschatological expectancy comes to expression in the fullest parallel of all, that with Elijah, the prophet awaited at the Last Times. Like Elijah in the prophecy of Malachi (Ml 3:1), John will go before the Lord and will reconcile parents to their children (as in Ml 3:24). The Annunciation of the birth of the Baptist is seen, therefore, as bringing the promises of God in the Old Testament to their climax.

With the annunciation to Zechariah the Annunciation to Mary shows a detailed parallel:

	Zechariah	*Mary*
Gabriel came	v. 11	v. 26
an awestruck reaction	v. 12	v. 29
'do not be afraid'	v. 13	v. 30
the promise of a son	v. 13	v. 31
a name given	v. 13	v. 31
he will be great	v. 15	v. 32
his task outlined	vv. 16–17	v. 33
a question	v. 18	v. 34
the angel responds	v. 19	v. 35

| a sign given | v. 20 | v. 36 |
| exit | v. 22 | v. 39 |

The differences between the two stories are, however, just as significant. If Mary is compared with Zechariah, three points may be noted.

1. Zechariah's worth is described in terms of observance of the Law. Mary's goes beyond this. The greeting to Mary, κεχαριτωμένη, conventionally translated 'full of grace', denotes the gift of God's unmerited and freely-bestowed favour. This grace or favour is like the unpredictable smile or choice of a favourite by an all-powerful despot; it is not earned, but is simply a matter of the free choice of the ruler.

2. Zechariah's question is seen as a reprehensible objection, doubting the message. Mary's question is simply on the means to be employed, and receives its answer in the presence and creative power of God, signified by the Holy Spirit coming upon her and in the overshadowing cloud.

3. Zechariah, naturally, gives no reply to the angel's last message. Mary replies as the Lord's Servant. This may be a reminiscence of the Servant Songs in Isaiah, which played such an important part in Jesus' own self-image. It certainly already presents Mary – as she will be seen in Luke (see page 144) – as the model disciple.

The chief comparison, however, is that between John and Jesus.

1. John will be 'great in the sight of the Lord', whereas Jesus will simply be 'great' without qualification. John will be the forerunner; Jesus will be the one heralded.

2. John will, like Samuel and Samson, be a nazirite, dedicated to the service of God. Jesus will be Son of the Most High. In view of the mention of the Holy Spirit overshadowing Mary, there may well be a reference to the early Christian confessional formula which lies behind Romans 1:4, 'in terms of the Spirit and of holiness was designated Son of God in power'. At any rate, this expression goes well beyond the Old Testament terms, to embrace the Christological confessions of the early Church.

3. John will fulfil the task of Elijah. Jesus will be the messianic king who was promised by Nathan to David in 2 S 7. This promise had been at the centre of Israel's hope for a millenium, adjusted, quoted, referred to constantly throughout the Bible. After 'his reign will have no end', nothing more can be added.

3 THE BIRTHS

The parallel between these two Narratives is not so detailed as in the case of the Annunciations; the story of the birth of the Baptist is too brief for that.

Elizabeth	Mary
'The time came for Elizabeth to have her child, and she gave birth to a son'	'The time came for her [Mary] to have her child, and she gave birth to a son'
Visit of the neighbours	Visit of the shepherds
Joy	Great joy

The significance of the birth of John becomes clear only in the following story of his circumcision and naming. Here there is an air of the mysterious hand of God. Elizabeth knows (without communication?) the name which the angel has selected. Zechariah's power of speech returns as soon as he ensures the fulfilment of the angel's command. All the onlookers are filled with astonishment, awe and wonder: 'What will this child turn out to be?'

The air is also filled with joy and with the praise of God. Both these features will be repeated at the birth of Jesus, only with greater intensity. The 'joy' (Lk 1:58) has become 'great joy' (2:10). The shepherds, like Elizabeth's relations, praise and glorify God, but in so doing they are only following the example of the hosts of heaven, who first have been 'praising God with the words "Glory to God in the highest heaven"' (2:14). The praise and joy have been translated onto a new level.

To readers alive to the resonances of the Old Testament the allusions to John's prophetic role continue, so that his story is seen to echo that of the Chosen People itself. 'The child grew' (1:80) is an echo of Isaac's growth (Gn 21:8). 'The hand of the Lord was with him' (1:66) echoes the youth of Samson and Samuel (Jg 13:24; 1 S 2:21).

The significance of the birth of Jesus, on the other hand, is written into the account itself. Of the many aspects we may delay perhaps on three.

The contrast with Caesar Augustus

Caesar Augustus lurks in the background. He is responsible for the census which brings Mary to Bethlehem, the destined birthplace of the Messiah of David. His edict for the census decrees to the world what the message of the angel decrees to God's faithful.

The census

The census has frequently been used in apologetics to show Luke's historical accuracy. This is no longer the case, for it bristles with historical difficulties.

Quirinius was governor of Syria in AD 6/7, which is far too late for Jesus' birth. It was at this later date that a census certainly took place, on the occasion of the transfer of rule over Judaea from Archelaus (King Herod's son) to direct Roman rule. Censuses of the provinces of the Roman Empire were a regular feature, taking place in different provinces at different times. But it is highly unlikely that a census took place while Herod was still king, and his kingdom still a 'client kingdom', not fully incorporated into the Empire. Under his kingship Judaea would not be liable to Roman taxes, which were an important purpose of a census.

The census at the time of Jesus' birth is therefore either a confused historical memory or 'a purely literary device', as Joseph Fitzmyer holds.[1] Even if the census at the time were correct, it would be unprecedented – and hard to envisage – that families should return to their ancestral homes.

Augustus was also the greatest ruler the world had yet known. Above all, he was responsible and famed for the Pax Romana, the peace which was universally hailed with joy and relief after decades of war and upheaval all over the Mediterranean world. The king born at Bethlehem to David's line was of a quite different kind, and the 'peace on earth' which his birth inaugurates was also different. The royal dignity of the child is hinted at in little ways. For instance, the swaddling clothes (Lk 2:7) echo Wisdom 7:4–5, when the author writes, in King Solomon's name:

> I was nurtured in swaddling clothes, with every care.
> No king has known any other beginning of existence

[1] Joseph A. Fitzmyer, *The Gospel According to Luke* [Anchor Bible series], New York, Doubleday, vol. 1, p. 393.

The poverty of Jesus

In accordance with Luke's message later in the gospel (see page 145), the stress is on Jesus coming in poverty, or even near-destitution, as is shown firstly by his cradle, a cattle trough.

No room at the inn

Popular pictures of the innkeeper turning away Joseph and Mary rest upon a misunderstanding of the Latin word used in St Jerome's translation, *diversorium*, usually rendered as 'inn'. The Greek word κατάλυμα has a quite different meaning: it suggests a large, probably split-level, space, the area where the people would live; the cattle would be in the same living-area, but perhaps on the lower level. Luke indicates that there was no room for the child in the area where humans dwelt, so that he had to be lodged with the cattle.

There may also be allusion to Jeremiah 14:8:

Yahweh, hope of Israel,
its Saviour in time of distress,
why are you like a stranger in this country,
like a traveller staying only for one night?

In the last line – 'a traveller lodging in a κατάλυμα' – the Greek word obviously indicates a provisional, unsatisfactory place to stay.

The retinue who greet this king are also the poor. It would not be justified to use later rabbinic legislation to classify the shepherds as unclean outcasts; but they are undoubtedly the poor, to whom Luke will later show Jesus so determinedly offering a welcome. There may also be allusion to the biblical image of those who care for the people – Yahweh or earthly rulers – as shepherds: the shepherds pay homage to the new-born Shepherd.

Titles given to Jesus

The quality of the child is shown also by the titles he is given, 'Saviour' and 'Christ the Lord'.

1. *'Saviour'* This is a title reserved in the Old Testament to Yahweh. In Job 19:25 God is so described: Job in the depths of his misery cries, 'I know that I have a living Defender/Redeemer/Saviour', using the Hebrew term גֹאֵל (*go'el*). This is a technical term of family law, the nearest male relative, who in certain circumstances is

bound to bail out and rescue his near relative; it expresses, therefore, a certain family closeness and loyalty under pressure. In Deutero-Isaiah this term is used of God frequently, expressing the certainty that he will release his people from exile in Babylon, just as he had freed Israel from captivity in Egypt (see Is 41:14, note g). In the New Testament the title of Saviour is transferred by Luke to Jesus (see the footnote on page 140). It is so used also in the Pastoral Letters (see 1 Tm 1:1, NJB note b) – that is, right at the end of the New Testament development. It indicates, therefore, the dependable, inalienable family love, protection and loyalty lavished by God on Israel. In the context of its use by Luke and the Pastoral Letters, both of which have strong links with the Hellenistic world, it may also contrast with the title of 'Saviour' by which the Roman emperor was commonly hailed, implying a claim that the true Saviour was not the emperor but Jesus.

2. *'The Lord'* This also is a divine title in the Old Testament, translating the sacred name יהוה (Yahweh) in the Greek version of the Bible. In the gospels it is used also overwhelmingly of God, though it occurs sparingly in Mark and Matthew of Jesus, usually in the vocative ('Lord!'), where it may mean no more than 'Sir!' Only when the article is used ('*the* Lord') does it have a clear fuller sense. Further, it is occasionally unclear whether it refers to God or to Jesus, for example when Jesus sends off the cured demoniac of Gerasa, commanding him to 'tell them all that the Lord in his mercy has done for you' (Mk 5:19) – is this Jesus, or God acting through Jesus? Luke, however, shows how he regards Jesus by frequently calling him '*the* Lord', transferring to Jesus what was normally a divine title. In the Acts 'those who invoke the name of the Lord' – meaning 'put themselves under the patronage of Christ as God' – is the technical term for Christians (see Acts 2:21, NJB note m). In the early years of the Church and of persecution, to call Jesus, rather than Caesar, 'the Lord' became the test of faith.

By these two titles, then, Luke shows clearly the Christology which will inspire the remainder of the gospel.

4 THE CANTICLES

The Magnificat

This first of the three canticles of the Infancy Story (Lk 1:46–55) expresses Mary's joy at her coming child and the salvation he is to bring. In assessing whether Luke composed the poem or adopted it, perhaps from some pre-existing Jewish-Christian hymn, it has been pointed out that only verse 48 need be specific to Mary (again describing herself as the Servant of the Lord, as at the Annunciation). But the principal theme of salvation promised to the lowly and unfortunate, the reversal of situations of the mighty and the lowly, is emphasised throughout this gospel.

The note of joy runs throughout the Infancy Narratives, and the fulfilment brought to Israel is also a central idea in both. So, whether it was composed by Luke or not, the canticle circles round theological themes which are dear to him. As so often in the Infancy Story, the theme of fulfilment of Old Testament promises is given by the similarity of the canticle to Hannah's song of thanksgiving for her child in 1 S 2. The canticle is also reminiscent of many of the psalms of thanksgiving and praise in the Old Testament and in the Qumran literature.

The pattern of the canticle is best seen as two double strophes, the first concerning Mary as an individual and the second the People of God. Each strophe begins with verbs of action, and is followed by peaceful reflection, relating the action to God's mercy to Israel.

> My soul proclaims the greatness of the Lord,
> and my spirit rejoices in God my Saviour;
> because he has looked upon the humiliation of his servant.
> Yes, from now onwards all generations will call me blessed,
> for the Almighty has done great things for me.
>
>> Holy is his name
>> and his faithful love extends age after age to those who fear
>> him.
>
> He has used the power of his arm,
> he has routed the arrogant of heart.
> He has pulled down princes from their thrones and raised high
> the lowly.
> He has filled the starving with good things, sent the rich away
> empty.
>
>> He has come to the help of Israel his servant, mindful of his
>> faithful love
>> – according to the promise he made to our ancestors – of his
>> mercy to Abraham and to his descendants for ever.

The Benedictus

The second of the three canticles (Lk 1:68–79) is inserted at the end of the story of John's circumcision and naming – 'inserted', because verses 67–79 can be removed with no diminution, but rather an improvement, of the flow of the narrative. Discussion has raged about its origin, whether it was composed by Luke himself, drawn from a Jewish hymn (with supplements) or from an earlier Jewish-Christian source. Two facts stand out: that in its present form it draws on the Greek rather than the Hebrew Bible, and that it expresses perfectly Luke's purpose and theology.

The dominant theme of the canticle is that God's promises to Israel have come to fulfilment, a message which Luke has been anxious to teach throughout the Infancy Narrative. This much is clear from the opening blessing (in the conventional style of psalms, used also at Qumran[2]), 'Blessed be the Lord God of Israel'; from the recurrence in verses 69–75 of the revered names of Israel, David and Abraham, of the prophets of old, and of the great keywords of the biblical tradition, such as 'his people', 'covenant' and 'faithful love'; and especially from the Lukan keyword 'salvation'.

Besides first looking backwards to the history of Israel, the canticle then (vv. 76–9) looks forward to the task of the child – the canticle is, after all, the answer to the question, 'What will this child turn out to be?' (v. 66) – namely, the prophetic role which will be seen later in the gospel: to prepare a way for the Lord and to prepare people for the forgiveness of sins, together with the lovely final image of light dawning in darkness. The continuity of John's task with God's preparation of his people for salvation in the Old Testament is emphasised by a repetition of the same keywords in the two halves of the canticle, 'his people', 'faithful love', and 'salvation'.

But there is also a note of sadness in Luke at Jesus' lack of success in this task with Israel. The same expressions recur in Jesus' lament over Jerusalem (19:42–4): the same 'enemies' are to destroy Jerusalem, which has failed to recognise 'the way to peace' at the time of its 'visitation'.

The Nunc Dimittis

The final canticle of the Infancy Narrative (Lk 2:29–32) is as redolent of the Old Testament as the others, and particularly of the promises of salvation in Deutero-Isaiah, to which several of the phrases allude. Its

---

[2] 1 QM 14:4: see Geza Vermes, *The Dead Sea Scrolls in English* (Harmondsworth, Penguin, 1962), p. 142.

keynote is the fulfilment of the promises to Israel as the source of salvation to the gentiles. Although it is so much shorter than the other canticles – only three short couplets – it evinces the same dependence on the Old Testament themes of salvation, peace and God's people Israel.

Luke's concept of salvation

Taken together, the three canticles give an overview of Luke's concept of salvation.

1. It is the fulfilment of the promises to Israel, granted to the poor of Yahweh, a reversal of the fortunes enjoyed by the rich and powerful – expressed pri.narily in the *Magnificat*.
2. It comes to expression through the prophetic Spirit seen in the agents of salvation, from John the Baptist, through Jesus, to the ministers of the early Church, who are guided by the Spirit of the Risen Christ – expressed primarily in the *Benedictus*.
3. It extends beyond the confines of Israel to all the nations – expressed primarily in the *Nunc Dimittis*.

Certainly it is possible that Luke used three songs which already existed in the Jewish Christian community. But his own literary skill and the precision with which the canticles accord with and express his own theology make it more probable that they are, like the rest of the Narrative, composed by himself.

5 PERSONAL STUDY

1. Write an essay: 'How does Luke's Infancy Story show the child Jesus to be already the Christ of Christianity?
2. Read everything you can on one or more of these canticles and write a short study of it or them: the arrangement, the theology, the authorship, and so on.

CHAPTER 17

THE RESURRECTION APPEARANCES

I THE EMPTY TOMB

The Markan account

The priority of Mark

Here the priority of Mark becomes really important, for his account is to be evaluated quite differently if he was the first to write such an account from the way it is evaluated if he wrote after Matthew and Luke. This discussion will be based on two propositions which at various times have been disputed:

1. Mark's account is the first which has come down to us.
2. Mark's gospel ends at Mark 16:8 (see page 71). That is, the texts sometimes printed after 16:8 are not part of the original gospel of Mark – they are in fact a catena of snippets from other gospels, the Acts, and other early Christian writings. In Mark's gospel proper there is no account of Resurrection appearances: once the accounts of Resurrection appearances in the other gospels and the events recounted in the Acts had become part of the written Christian message, it was felt that Mark was incomplete, and verses 16:9–20 (and an alternative shorter addition) were fitted onto the end of the gospel.

To modern Christians the striking feature of Mark's account (Mk 16:1–8) is that the narrative of the Empty Tomb is not an apologetic proof text. The women make no attempt to verify what the angel has told them about the emptiness of the tomb; this they would have done if the object of the account were to prove that the tomb was truly empty: 'On entering the tomb they saw' – not that the tomb was empty, but – 'a young man in a white robe . . .'. Far from verifying the fact, they came out and ran away. The fact that the tomb was empty is taken for granted, and all the accent of the account is on the *meaning* of this. It is treated as an accepted fact which needs not to be proved but to be explained.

The accent of the account is partly on the explanation given in the angel's message that the Risen Christ has gone before them into Galilee, but more especially on the reaction of the women. Dominating the account is their fear, awe and amazement. In three verses this is stated four times: 'they were struck with amazement', 'There is no need to be so amazed', 'they were frightened out of their wits', 'for they were afraid' (the last words of the gospel). The words used for this fear and amazement are those used for the reaction to a divine happening or to the presence of the divine. In thus narrating the incident Mark is showing the reader that the divine has entered history in a new way. The general resurrection of the dead at the end of time was a normal belief among the Jews (though still not accepted by the Sadducees), but what staggered and frightened the women was that the end-time, and God's action at the end-time, had suddenly come upon them. The final presence of God had entered history. It is on this note that Mark's gospel ends: for him this was the meaning of the Resurrection (see pages 71–3).

The Lukan account

As so often, Luke in his account (Lk 24:1–12) stresses some aspects which Mark had not emphasised.

Luke's concern for proof
The women do check that the tomb is empty: 'they could not find the body'. In all the accounts Luke is more concerned with definite proof, and primarily physical proof, of the reality of the Resurrection. As he insists that the Spirit comes down at the Baptism 'in bodily form' like a dove, and in physical tongues of fire at Pentecost, so he will insist in the Resurrection Appearances on the physical nature of Christ's body.

The importance of the women
Again Luke gives to the women more value and importance, as he has done to them and especially to Mary throughout the gospel (see pages

143–4). In Mark they do not pass on the message; in Luke the women are the first to pass on the message of the Resurrection, and it is the Eleven who refuse to believe. Even when Peter himself goes to check (24:12) he is merely amazed, and does not come to explicit faith.

The emphasis on Jerusalem

For Luke the Resurrection Appearances are going to be in and around Jerusalem. He therefore needs subtly to reverse the message of the angel that 'he is going ahead of you to Galilee; that is where you will see him, just as he told you' (Mk 16:7). This is neatly done, still with the mention of Galilee, but in a quite different way: 'Remember what he told you when he was still in Galilee' (Lk 24:6). So the reference is no longer to the saying on the way to Gethsemane (Mk 14:28), but to the three great prophecies of the Passion and the Resurrection (e.g. Lk 9:22).

The fulfilment of prophecy

This further enables Luke to stress once again the message of prophecy and fulfilment: 'the Son of man was destined to be handed over . . . and rise again on the third day' (see page 135).

2 THE ROAD TO EMMAUS

This is another of Luke's beautifully told stories (Lk 24:13–35), and one vital for explaining the process of evangelisation, the passing on and explanation of the Good News of the Resurrection. Jesus is the first to explain the Resurrection, and – as Luke himself has done and will do in the Acts – he explains it in terms of the Old Testament prophecies; it is these prophecies which make sense of and give meaning to the events of Jesus' life, ministry, death and Resurrection. It is only after this explanation that the disciples recognise the stranger for what he is. The explanation leads on to the shared meal, at which the recognition of Jesus actually takes place. This in its turn is the forerunner of the community meal, the sacrament of the eucharist.

The story is told with all Luke's skill of characterisation and surprise. The disciples are depressed, 'their faces downcast', and tell their story with a dull wistfulness in their disappointment at the failure of their hopes. This turns to excitement as they agree 'Did not our hearts burn within us . . .?' and they 'set out that instant'. The elements of suspense and surprise, so prominent in the Hellenistic novels (see page 112), are woven into the gospel message in a masterly fashion.

The extent to which Luke has himself formed the story is shown by a comparison with the story of the baptism of the Ethiopian in Acts 8:26–40. This, too, has the explanation of Jesus' role by means of scripture, leading to enlightenment and a sacrament (baptism) – an example of the *kerygma* in action. It, too, has the lively dialogue and the surprise elements of sudden appearance and disappearance. Each begins with a journey and a meeting, and ends with a separation and a further journey. Each story has the same pattern, built on a chiasmus to emphasise the message at the centre. Luke 24:

> **a** from Jerusalem
>> **b** talking together
>>> **c** Jesus came up
>>>> **d** eyes prevented
>>>>> **e** hope
>>>>>> **f** went to tomb
>>>>>>> **g alive**
>>>>>> **f′** went to tomb
>>>>> **e′** fulfilment of hope
>>>> **d′** eyes opened
>>> **c′** Jesus vanished
>> **b′** they said to each other
> **a′** to Jerusalem

Acts 8:

> **a** on his journey
>> **b** the Spirit acts
>>> **c** Philip ran up
>>>> **d** joint action
>>>>> **e good news of Jesus**
>>>> **d′** joint action
>>> **c′** Philip taken away
>> **b′** the Spirit acts
> **a′** on his journey

The major difference, of course, is that before the Ascension Jesus is the moving force, whereas after the Ascension it is his Spirit.

3 THE APPEARANCE IN JERUSALEM

Luke's account of the final appearance of the Risen Christ in Jerusalem brings his gospel to a fitting conclusion, preparing for the Acts of the

Apostles which is to follow. It has striking similarities to John's account of an appearance to the disciples in the upper room, with the marked difference that in Luke there is no gift of the Spirit; this is reserved till the scene of Pentecost which initiates the mission of the Church. In Luke the Risen Christ's last instructions are to wait for this occasion. The riches of this last account may be considered under three heads.

The fulfilment of prophecy

The gospel ends as it began, with the message of scripture. Jesus once again explains the meaning of his work in terms of the Old Testament. Without such a background it is impossible to understand what Jesus meant; this has been the lesson in each of the instructions of the Resurrection incidents, and will be the theme of the instructions throughout the teaching of the Acts. The whole gospel has been constructed to demonstrate this theme of prophecy and fulfilment.

It is not without significance that the gospel ends with two allusions to great figures of the prophetic Old Testament.

1. Jesus' ascension into heaven is reminiscent primarily of the departure of Elijah to heaven in a fiery chariot (2 K 2:11). Elijah leaves behind him, in the form of his cloak, a double share of his Spirit on his follower Elisha. Just so Luke deliberately uses the metaphor that his witnesses are to be 'clothed with' the Spirit which the Father has promised. There must also be a reminiscence of Moses, who was also taken to God from a mountaintop (Mount Nebo), whose tomb was unknown, and who left his work to his successor, Joshua, who 'was filled with the spirit of wisdom, for Moses had laid his hands upon him' (Dt 34:9).

2. The gesture of the final solemn blessing, 'raising his hands he blessed them', must also be reminiscent of Aaron's blessing following the instructions of Moses (Lv 9:22). It will surely also recall the wonderful picture of the blessing by the High Priest Simon Onias with which Ecclesiasticus, the Book of Ben Sira, concludes (Si 50:20): a magnificent description, ending

> Then he would come down and raise his hands
>   over the whole assembly of the Israelites,
> to give them the Lord's blessing from his lips

The full reality of the Risen Christ

Luke insists on both the continuity of the Risen Lord with the Jesus whom they had known, and the difference between them. In a purely Jewish environment there was no need to insist on the bodily reality of the Risen Christ, for in biblical anthropology no continuance of life could be conceived other than as an animated body. It was only in the sphere of Greek philosophy, with its analysis of the human condition into body and soul, that continuance of life as a ghost, a sort of disembodied soul, could be conceived.

Ideals about the life after death

In an earlier stage of development of doctrine, when the dead were envisaged as continuing in Sheol, their life there was conceived as a disembodied flitting, a powerless inactivity amid dust and darkness which was the very negation of life. This has little relationship to any Christian conception of the living power of the Risen Christ.

Luke is writing, however, for a Hellenistic readership: to convey the full reality of the Risen Christ, therefore, he needs to insist on the bodily reality. (Similarly at the Baptism he stresses that the Holy Spirit descended 'in bodily form' like a dove.) It was for this reason that he tells us that the women checked the emptiness of the tomb. So now Christ demonstrates to them his hands and his feet, inviting them to touch him and stressing that 'a ghost has no flesh and bones as you can see I have' (Lk 24:39), and takes and eats a piece of what Luke so vividly describes as 'grilled fish'.

The disciples' awe

At the same time it is clear that the Risen Christ is not the earthly companion whom they knew. The disciples on the way to Emmaus had at first failed to recognise him. The disciples now also are 'agitated', 'in a state of alarm and fright', 'dumbfounded', and still could not believe it – with the lame Lukan excuse that 'their joy was so great' (compare 22:45, where their collapse is excused on the opposite but psychologically similar grounds of 'grief'). These reactions are basically those of awe at the presence of something beyond their comprehension, something divine.

This leads directly on to their final act of worship of the Risen Lord: 'They worshipped him and then went back to Jerusalem full of joy' (24:52). This is tantamount to a full confession of the divinity of the Risen Christ, for Luke here uses the verb προσκυνέω, which he understands strictly only of divine worship: 'You must worship the Lord your God, him alone you must serve' (4:8).

The stage is now set for the coming of the Spirit and the spread of the message of the Risen Christ from Jerusalem to the ends of the earth.

4 PERSONAL STUDY

Write a brief reflection on what following and working through this book has contributed to your understanding of the gospel.